Torah for the Nations

Commentary on the weekly Torah readings from the
Five Books of Moses, with lessons for peoples of all nations,
backgrounds and beliefs

I0147546

by

Rabbi Avraham Greenbaum

Edited by Nachum Shaw

Promised Land

JERUSALEM   LONDON   NEW YORK

Copyright © 2019 by AVRAHAM GREENBAUM

ISBN 978-09956560-9-3

All rights reserved. No part of this publication may be reproduced or transmitted in any form or by any means, electronic or mechanical, including photocopying, recording, or any information storage or retrieval system, without the prior permission of the publishers.

For further information:

Promised Land Publishers

Apt. 8, 5 Gimmel Alroyi St.

Jerusalem 9210808

ISRAEL

or

Promised Land Publishers

8 Woodville Road

London NW11 9TN

ENGLAND

or

Promised Land Publishers

67 Wood Hollow Lane

New Rochelle

NY 10804

USA

Email: promisedland920@gmail.com

www.promisedlandpublishers.com

Torah

for the

Nations

Commentary on the weekly Torah readings from the Five Books of Moses, with lessons for peoples of all nations, backgrounds and beliefs

"And many people shall come and say, 'Come let us go up to the mountain of Hashem, to the House of the God of Jacob, and He will teach of His ways, and we will walk in His paths.'"

ISAIAH 2:3

GENESIS

EXODUS

LEVITICUS

NUMBERS

DEUTERONOMY

Torah Study and the Dignity of Man

Going around in circles

My head is still spinning from the festival of Succot, which we celebrated all last week. On each morning of the first days of the festival we made a one-circuit procession around the synagogue Torah reading desk carrying our palm branches, citrons, myrtle and willow branches ("the four kinds", Leviticus 23:40) chanting prayers. On the morning of the seventh day, we made *seven* circuits. That night, the eve of the eighth day, we took out all the Torah scrolls from the ark and carried them around the synagogue in seven series of circuits to the accompaniment of happy singing and dancing. We did the same the following morning, dancing more and more circles... Then we concluded the annual cycle of the reading of the Five Books of Moses - and immediately afterwards went back to the beginning to start the new cycle: "In the beginning, God created the Heaven and the Earth" (Gen. 1:1).

A circle has no beginning or end, and likewise the divine wisdom contained in God's Torah is never-ending, infinite.... We humans, however, are finite creatures: we need to start somewhere and to know that we are headed to some destination or end point. Thus, the Torah has a beginning and an end. Yet as soon as we reach the end (Deuteronomy 34:12), we cycle right back to the beginning again, because the Torah, like a circle, goes on forever.

Ancient Jewish tradition ordains that the time for ending the annual Torah-reading cycle and beginning afresh comes after the spiritual heights of the "Days of Awe" (the New Year and Day of Atonement, September-October), at the climax of the ensuing joyous Succot festival on the "Eighth Day of Solemn Assembly" (Leviticus 23:36): "Simchat Torah", "Rejoicing of the Torah". (Outside the land of Israel this is held on the 9th day of the festival).

Good resolutions: A regular study schedule

This is a season of renewal and a time for good resolutions. Thus, many students and lovers of the Torah use this season to strengthen their commitment to a regular schedule of Torah study covering not only the weekly Torah portion, Prophets and Holy Writings (the Bible, "TaNaCh") but also other fundamental Torah literature. Each person makes his or her own schedule according to their level of knowledge, area of interest and availability of time. Even if one can find only a few minutes here and there out of a busy day to open or browse a Torah work, this alone, shines light, wisdom and blessing into our lives.

In this world we are exposed to a multitude of often confusing messages and influences, some positive, others highly negative. Within ourselves our minds and hearts are sometimes assailed with conflicting thoughts and feelings. We desperately need a source of true guidance as to how to follow a life-path that can bring us to genuine, lasting happiness.

This source of guidance is the Torah - a book, or rather a literature that you read not just once but study and review over and over again. For only through regular study and review do our knowledge and understanding of God's Wisdom increase and remain in our minds and hearts. Torah study is one of the three things on which the world stands, the other two being prayer and acts of kindness (Pirkey Avot 1:2).

Should gentiles study the Torah?

The Torah was specifically given to the Children of Israel to guard and observe, and many of its commandments apply only to those who are members of the people of Israel, whether by birth or through voluntary, lawful conversion. At the same time the Torah is full of teachings that apply to all mankind, especially the Seven Universal Laws, and it is a treasury of eternal wisdom, guidance, love and compassion for all.

1. Every gentile is obligated to learn and understand the Seven Universal Laws, which apply to all people. Under Noahide law, a gentile may be

executed for unintentionally violating one of the Seven Laws through ignorance, because he should have learned (Talmud, Maccot 9; Bava Kama 91).

2. Every gentile is commanded to know HaShem (Introduction to Talmud by Rav Nissim Gaon, 990-1062).

3. It is forbidden for a gentile to study those portions of the Torah that apply only to the people of Israel as members of the Covenant obligated to observe all 613 Commandments of the Torah specifically given to Israel. According to the Talmud, a gentile who studies those portions would be liable to death from Heaven (Sanhedrin 59a). This would apply to depth study of the Talmud and Kabbalah, for the proper understanding of which years of preparation are required. Without these, such study can be dangerous for the student and possibly for many others around him or her. Any gentile who sincerely wishes to make a deep study of Talmud or the original Kabbalistic texts should first convert.

4. It is permitted for a gentile to study those of the 613 commandments for Israelites that a gentile may observe voluntarily without converting. Later commentaries in this book will set forth what these commandments are.

5. Other Torah and works that gentiles may study with benefit and without danger would include the Bible and works on the fundamentals of Torah faith, belief and ethical self-improvement by

acknowledged rabbinical authorities, including Rabbi Moses Maimonides ("Rambam", 1135-1204), Rabbi Moshe Chayim Luzzatto ("Ramchal", 1707-47), Rabbi Shneur Zalman of Liadi, the first Lubavitcher Rebbe (1745-1812), and Rabbi Nachman of Breslov (1772-1810).

Make time

As we celebrate the first Shabbat after the festivals and embark on our journey through the New Year, let us carry with us the lesson of the dance circles of Simchat Torah. All of us, Jew and Gentile, each in our own way, must "carry the Torah around with us" as we pursue our lives each day of the annual cycle - by setting ourselves regular times to study the Torah during the day and during the week, each according to our own unique life situation.

In Hebrew, a Torah study session is called a **shiur**, which means a "measure". For different people the measure - a paragraph, a page, several pages, a chapter or more - must necessarily be different. What is important is that each one gets his or her daily portion of all the spiritual vitamins, minerals and other nutrients that nourish the soul. For "the Torah of HaShem is perfect, restoring the soul" (Psalms 19:8).

Your regular "measure" of Torah, be it a few minutes each day, a weekly or bi-weekly class or more, will bring more to your life than many forms of entertainment. It also usually costs much less money! For the Torah is acquired not with money but through devotion.

The Ark and the Word

Torah speaks in the language of humans

A fundamental principle of rabbinic Torah interpretation is that "the Torah speaks in the language of humans" (Baal HaTurim on Numbers 15:31 etc.). Surely this could not mean that the Divine Writ would use language in the sloppy, imprecise, sensationalist or hyper-clever ways that language is too often used today in everyday chatter, the media, politics and other public forums!

As God's revelation to humanity, the Torah speaks in terms, concepts and ideas that have meaning to humans as they ostensibly relate to the familiar world around us. Torah speaks about all the various situations of human life - life-cycle, family and social relations, agriculture, making a living, war, peace and countless others. Indeed, the lessons we learn are to be practically applied in our actual lives. Simultaneously, the Torah is providing us with metaphors and allegories that help us gain a little grasp of spiritual levels that are intrinsically beyond our understanding during the present incarnation of our souls in our bodies.

Through the subtle weave of its tales and teachings, the Torah - the Tree of Life - nourishes our souls in preparation for the life beyond this life, among whose rewards is that we shall be given to know and understand what we sought earnestly to understand during our lives in this world. A small child may become absorbed in the Bible stories while elders and sages fathom ever deeper. The four levels of rabbinic interpretation are called PaRDeS ("orchard", "Paradise") standing for **P'shat**, the "simple" meaning of the text; **Remez**, its allusive meaning; **Drash**, the homiletic, allegorical level, and **Sod**, the secret, mystical and esoteric level including mathematical equations, encrypted ciphers and much more.

Rabbi Shlomo Yitzchaki (1040-1105), prince of the Biblical commentators, universally known as **Rashi**, which is the acronym of the initial letters of his name, states a fundamental principle of Torah interpretation: "The Torah never leaves its **P'shat**" (Rashi on Gen. 15:10, Exodus 12:2). That is to say: besides any other levels of meaning it may have, each verse means exactly what it says in simple terms. Yet this "simple" meaning is not necessarily identical with what some might consider the "literal" meaning (which sometimes seems ridiculous and impossible). Likewise, many of the metaphors in constant use in everyday speech communicate simply and directly even though we know they cannot be taken absolutely "literally". Likewise, the stories in the Bible happened and are continuing to happen until today, but *how* they happened and are happening may be very different from what we might imagine. Ever since Moses gave the Torah to

Israel, its lovers have spent lifetimes delving beneath first-sight impressions to deeper meanings. In the words of the Mishnaic sage known as Ben Bag Bag: "Turn it over and turn it over, for all is in it" (Pirkey Avot 5:22)

Noah's flood

Many scholars in the last few hundred years have dismissed the Torah account of Noah's Flood as a myth having no higher status than several parallel stories handed down in various other ancient cultures. But assiduous students of the original Hebrew text of the Torah see it plainly to be a perfectly chiseled Divine document embedded with multiple levels and lessons that apply at all times, past, present and future.

Contemporary culture's intoxication with its technological achievements coupled with an appalling ignorance of history have led many to assume that prior to somewhere around 1750, human civilization was hopelessly primitive, not to speak of back in Biblical times. This flies in the face of clear evidence that the ancients possessed staggering knowledge of mathematics and astronomy as well as knowhow in agriculture, building and engineering, medicine and much more, as can be seen from relics like the excavated walls of the Temple Mount in Jerusalem, the Stonehenge astronomical-religious stone circle in southwest Britain and countless archeological finds.

Thus, the Holy Zohar (Bereishit 56a) states that the people in the generation of Noah's Flood possessed deep understanding of the use of magic, witchcraft and sorcery to control heavenly forces. What this means is that they knew formulas and ritual processes (comparable to some of the "wizardry" of modern science and technology?) through which they thought they could control the very elements of creation and master the world. This led them to an overweening, God-denying arrogance which caused the social fabric to deteriorate to a level where unashamed sexual immorality, blatant theft and robbery and other forms of wickedness were rampant, with the breakdown of all the limits and boundaries that are the necessary foundations of a God-aware civilization.

Noah's greatness lay in the fact that he was history's first Righteous Rebel. He defied the degeneracy and wickedness of his Godless age. To escape them, Noah, the father of humanity, took refuge in his " Ark ".

The Ark - the Word: Prayer

What really is this " Ark " that is described in such detail in our Torah portion? The Biblical Hebrew term **teivah** that is translated as Noah's " Ark " or ship denotes simply and "literally" a **container**, particularly what we might call a linguistic **container** - i.e. a **word**. For a word is a **container** of **meaning**. The **word** in which Noah took refuge from the surrounding wickedness is prayer, which is made up of **words** (Rabbi Nachman, Likutey Moharan Part I Teachings 9 and 112 translated in *Tsohar*, pub. Breslov Research Institute.) Noah's lesson to all humanity, his descendants in all the generations, is to pray. For Prayer is the second of the three things on which the world stands, together with Torah, as discussed in last week's commentary on Bereishit, and Acts of Kindness (Avot 1:20).

One of the primary lessons of the story of Noah's ark is that if we feel surrounded by the floodwaters of rampant materialism, degeneracy and other evils, we may find refuge by bringing all that is dear and important to us into our **prayer** to the Ruler of the Universe.

From early childhood we learn words and language as the means of communication between one human and another. Yet from the baby's first entry into this world, it instinctively cries a great cry to God. While the surrounding matrix of family, education and culture initiate the child into the world of human communication, secular culture teaches little about how to refine and elevate this incoherent cry to the level of a thoughtful, intelligent communication with our Maker using WORDS. Yet Prayer -- talking to God directly, expressing all our thoughts, feelings, needs and wants - is the logical corollary of the first of the Seven Universal Laws of Noah's children and descendants: the prohibition of idolatry. If idolatry is the denial of God's omnipotence, prayer to God is the affirmation that everything is in God's hands.

Idolatry is any form of religious service centered on the propitiation of one or more intermediary gods, angels, souls, forces or other powers rather than turning to the One Creator. Our destinies are ultimately governed not by the god of this or that or by fate or luck, nor by our boss, doctor, prime minister or any other human, but by God alone. We attain our greatest dignity as God's children when even as we seek to manipulate the material world through our own efforts in making a living, getting cured through medicines and attaining other goals, etc., at the same time we turn directly to God, Ruler of all, through our prayers so as to draw God's blessing on all our endeavors.

There is a widespread childish conception of prayer as asking for the magical fulfillment of a wish list that may range from houses, luxuries and winning the lottery to making granny better. But mature prayer is when we use words as a means of communication with God and with our own selves in order to clarify our goals and purpose in this life and to help us attain them. God has given each one his or her own soul, self and unique life situation, and He has also given us the ability to develop, change and refine ourselves. We must ask God to help us overcome innate laziness, heaviness, excessive materialistic involvements and other personal weaknesses. The generic Hebrew word for prayer, **tefilah**, comes from the root **palal** meaning to judge. The Hebrew verb to "pray", **hitpalel**, is grammatically a reflexive form of the root. This is because in true prayer we judge ourselves and examine where we fall short, and we turn to our Creator to help us improve. The Torah teaches "to serve Him with all your hearts and all your souls" (Deuteronomy 11:13). "What is the service of God that is in the heart? It is Prayer!" (Ta'anit 2a).

What sacrifices does God want?

We humans are made of two sides: (1) The physical, animal body, which is vitalized by the "animal" soul that manifests in our this-worldly ego; (2) The life-giving spiritual soul, which gives us the dignified ability, apparently not shared with animals and other living creatures, to be self-aware and to elevate ourselves so as to earn closeness with God through our own efforts. Torah teachings set goals for our self-development, while our way to attain these goals is through an interactive "dialogue" with God where we do our part by praying and God responds as God sees fit in wisdom, love and compassion.

Our Torah portion tells us that after Noah came out of his Ark of Prayer into the new world washed clean of the old atheism by the waters of the Flood, he offered God burned offerings of animals and birds (Genesis 8:20). Was Noah teaching his descendants to offer such sacrifices?

The Torah does indeed command Israel to offer specific communal and personal physical animal, bird, meal, oil and wine sacrifices in the Temple in Jerusalem. Under Torah law a gentile may also send sacrifices to the Temple. Moreover, unlike an Israelite, a gentile may set up an altar to offer a burned offering elsewhere too, though this should only be done under the instruction of a competent Torah scholar (Rambam, Laws of Offering Sacrifices – *Maaseh Hakorbanot* 19:16). The Torah in no way gives sanction to practice animal sacrificial rituals other than those which it specifies.

But are animal sacrifices what God really wants of you and me? "To obey is better than sacrifice, and to listen better than the fat of rams" (I Samuel 15:22; cf. Isaiah 66:3).

Slaughtering the evil inclination

The sacrifice God wants is that we "slaughter" our evil inclination by bringing our negative traits and desires under control so that we develop our positive sides and fulfill our soul's true destiny in this world.

The way to "slaughter" our "bad side" is through the discipline - "service" - of regular prayer. This way we "sacrifice" our animal side to God and turn ourselves into true servants of God. "Take with you words and return to God...for bullock sacrifices we shall pay the offerings of our lips" (Hosea 14:3). "O God, open my lips and my mouth shall declare your praise. For You do not desire a sacrificial offering, or I would give it, You will not want a burnt offering. The sacrifices of God are a broken spirit; God will not despise a broken and contrite heart" (Psalms 51:17-19).

In the words of the outstanding Chassidic luminary, Rabbi Nachman of Breslov (1772-1810):

"You must pray for everything. Even if your garment is torn and you need another, you should pray to God to give you something to wear.

"Do this for everything; make it a habit to pray for all your needs, great or small. Your main prayers should be for fundamentals; that God should help you to serve Him and draw closer. Even so, you should also pray for minor things.

"God may give you food and clothing and everything else you need in life even without your asking for them. However, you are then like an animal. God provides all living creatures with their food. But if you do not draw your needs through prayer, your livelihood is like that of an animal. A man must draw his vitality and all his needs from God only through prayer.

"Is it beneath your dignity to pray even for something minor? You must pray for everything, even the most minor things" (Sichot Haran #233).

Rabbi Nachman here explains how to fulfill Noah's lesson to all his children, the 70 Nations of the World, in taking refuge in the "Ark" - the Word; to bring everything in our lives, our affairs and our very selves into our prayers to God.

The Milk of Human Kindness

Many of the Torah's most important teachings for all humanity come to us not in the form of laws and directives but embedded in story form, as in the cycle of stories of the three patriarchs, Abraham, Isaac and Jacob, which begins with our present portion of Lech Lecha. The lessons that come from the figure of Abraham are especially universal, as God Himself testifies in explaining the significance of his Hebrew name: "I have given you as father of a multitude of nations". Not only is Abraham the founding father of the people of Israel through his son Isaac and grandson Jacob. He is also the father of all the nations, because Abraham's oldest son, Ishmael, and his grandson, Esau, are each considered the leader of thirty-five of the seventy nations of the world.

Abraham came to teach the world how to love God, Who calls him "My beloved" (Isaiah 41:8). Abraham is the archetypal human embodiment of God's attribute of expansive Kindness (Chessed), and this may be discerned as the common theme of all that Abraham does. The Torah sages expressed this by saying that Abraham served as the "chariot" of God's Kindness, which "rode" upon him so as to be revealed in all the world on account of Abraham's perfect emulation of this attribute.

Kindness is the third of the "three things upon which the world stands" (Pirkey Avot 1:2), together with Torah study (see our commentary on Bereishit) and Prayer (see commentary on Noah. "The world is built on kindness" (Psalms 59:3).

Imitatio Dei

God is intrinsically good, and the nature of goodness is expansive - to bestow good upon others. "God is good to all" (Psalms 146:9). Since God is the ultimate good, the greatest goodness and kindness to His creations is to enable them to partake of God's goodness. This is possible when we humans strive to emulate His ways and thereby incorporate His attributes in our own souls and personalities (see Rabbi Moshe Chayim Luzzatto, "The Way of God" Part 1).

God's plan is to reveal Himself to all the world and teach His creations to partake of His goodness by following His ways. To accomplish this plan, He bestowed upon Abraham a unique soul that instinctively yearned and craved to understand the meaning and purpose of the universe. Abraham's unflinching quest to discover the Source of all things led him to the conclusion that there is but One Creator and Ruler over all: Him alone is it fitting to serve.

Thus, Abraham followed his ancestor Noah in turning to be a righteous rebel against the God-denying wickedness of his age. Abraham famously smashed his father Terach's idols and defied the aggressive world tyrant-leader, Nimrod, who cast Abraham into the furnace in Ur of the Chaldees (Nehemiah 9:7).

Following his miraculous delivery from the furnace, Abraham distanced himself from Nimrod and his corrupt culture, but unlike Noah, who did not try to save the rest of the world from disaster, Abraham set himself to repay his debt to God for being redeemed by striving to draw the rest of the world under His wings.

Rabbi Nachman of Breslov taught:

"Abraham would come into a city and run about crying, 'Woe! Woe!' and people would run after him the way they chase a madman. He would argue with them at length, trying to show them they were all caught up in a profoundly mistaken way of thinking. He was quite familiar with all the arguments and rationalizations they used to justify their idolatry. He used to demonstrate the falsity of their ideas and reveal the truths of faith. Some of the young people were attracted to him. He never even tried to draw older people closer because they were already firmly entrenched in their false beliefs and it would have been very hard to get them to change. It was the younger people who were drawn after him: they ran after him. He would go from city to city and they would run after him..." (Tzaddik #395).

Thus when Abraham "took Sarai his wife and Lot, son of his brother, and all the possessions they had acquired **and the souls they had made in Haran**" (Genesis 12:5), the Targum (Aramaic translation/commentary on Torah) explains that the latter were the converts he and Sarah had made: Abraham would talk to the men and Sarah to the women. They had hundreds of followers, of whom the most notable was Abraham's servant Eliezer (Gen. 15:2), who by tradition was Nimrod's son.

Love and fear of God

At the beginning of the comprehensive "Mishneh Torah" Code of Torah law, Rambam (Moses Maimonides, 1135-1204) writes:

"The Torah commands us to love and fear God: 'And you shall love the Lord your God' (Deut. 6:5); 'Revere the Lord your God' (ibid. 6:13). And what is the way to love Him and revere Him? At the time when a person contemplates His works and His wondrous, great creations and through them sees God's incomparable, endless wisdom, the person is instantly filled with love and praise and is overwhelmed by a great craving to know the great God, as David said, 'My soul thirsts for God, the living God' (Psalms 42:3). And as the person dwells on these very matters he immediately retreats in fear, realizing that he is a tiny, lowly, dark creature standing with minimal superficial understanding before the One that has perfect knowledge. As David said: 'When I see Your heavens, the work of Your fingers, what is man that you take him into account?'" (Psalms 8:5; Rambam, Mishneh Torah, Hilchot Yesodey HaTorah, Foundations of the Torah 2:1).

Encouraging us to study and ponder the wonders of creations and its workings, Rambam continues:

"When man contemplates these matters and recognizes all the different levels of God's creations, from the angels and the heavenly spheres to man and other creatures, and when he sees the wisdom of the Holy One blessed be He in all His works and creations, this increases his love of God and his soul thirsts and his flesh longs to love God and to stand in awe and fear on account of his lowliness and insignificance. and he finds that he is like a vessel filled with shame and disgrace, empty and lacking" (Rambam ibid. 4:12).

Through Abraham's miraculous delivery from Nimrod's furnace (archetype of the later redemption of his descendants from slavery in Egypt), he came to recognize God not only as the original Creator of the Universe but also as its ever-watchful Ruler, Who controls every detail of all that is happening constantly. Abraham realized that he was beholden to God for his freedom and his very life. He knew that he must devote himself entirely to His service. That is why he went around seeking to bring others to God, and Abraham introduced the world to the concept of serving God.

What is true kindness

One of the most important components of serving God is the practice of true kindness. This is not necessarily the same as trying to be "nice" to everyone and handing out candies and cookies. Politeness, good manners, a smiling face and the offer of a helping hand wherever possible all contribute to a humane civilization. However, it is necessary to distinguish between helping the people we like and members of our own group as opposed to the altruistic bestowal of true, unstinting kindness upon all without discrimination.

Thus, the Torah sages pointed out that the stork is in Hebrew called **chassidah** because she shows kindness (**chessed**) in sharing her food with others. Nevertheless, she is an impure species of bird because she only shows favor to her own kind (Leviticus 11:19; Chullin 63a). However, God extends His kindness to **all** His creatures, to the righteous, the intermediates and even to the wicked. Many times, we are required to help those we find alien and even repugnant (though certainly not to support the wicked in their wickedness). The giver of kindness and charity may not particularly like or love the needy recipient or the way he looks and behaves, yet he still has a duty to try to help him.

Among the forms of kindness listed by the Torah sages are:

1. Giving non-interest monetary loans to those in need. Providing someone with a non-interest loan is considered an even greater form of kindness than giving them an outright gift of charity to cover their immediate needs, because the loan enables them to establish a long-term means of independent livelihood in an honorable way.

2. Hospitality to wayfarers. Welcoming guests in one's home is considered greater than welcoming the Divine Presence (Talmud, Shabbat 127a).

3. Providing the requirements of needy brides and grooms, enabling them to set up a home and rear a new generation of worthy humans.

4. Mediation: Making peace between warring parties or individuals, and particularly between husbands and wives.

5. Burying the dead (i.e. attending their funerals). This is called the Kindness of Truth as the one who practices this can expect no repayment from the dead person!

The greatest kindness of all is to help others attain the truest good in the world: connection with God. But this cannot be achieved by force, and nowhere do we see that Abraham made people convert to his faith under the threat of being put to the sword if they refused. Faith in the true God has validity only if people are allowed to come to it of their own free will. Abraham surely used every possible argument to persuade people to come to the right conclusion, but more than anything he taught through his own personal example.

The milk of kindness

It may be ideal to flow out to others with unstinting kindness, but as humans our ability to do this is limited. Moreover, true kindness must be attenuated to the needs of the recipient in order that he or she should not be overwhelmed. Mother's milk is a universal symbol of kindness because it is perfectly attuned to the needs of the new, growing baby - yet only in the right quantities and only for a time. As the child grows, milk alone is insufficient. Children may crave sweets and candies but it is no kindness at all to pander to all their desires, which can be very harmful.

Being kind does not mean you have to be soft. People often do not care to dwell on the fact that life comes to an end with death, but it is a great kindness to make them aware that our time in this world is limited and that we should use it to acquire merits that will stand for us in the everlasting life after life. It is kind to people to help them understand that their actions are likely to have long-term consequences, and that they need to make wise choices. Where appropriate, it is a great kindness to reprove others for their unwise choices and bad behavior, as long as we do so with tact and sensitivity. "Good is open rebuke that stems from hidden love" (Proverbs 27:5). "He who spares the rod hates his son, but one who loves him chastises him regularly" (ibid. 13:24).

Liberal sentiment generally tends to oppose any kind of strictness not only in disciplining children but even in punishing delinquents, criminals, terrorists and mass murderers. Yet the Torah teaches that appropriate chastisement of wrongdoers is necessary both for the welfare of the wider society and for the wrongdoers' own long-term benefit (Rashi on Deuteronomy 21:18). The Torah sages have taught us that one who shows kindness to those who are cruel ends up being cruel to those who are kind (Meiri on Yoma 22b).

God chose Abraham because "I know him that he will instruct his children and his household after him and they will guard the way of God to practice charity and justice, in order that God should bring upon Abraham all that He has said about him" (Genesis 18:19).

All who follow the pathway that Abraham taught are called the people of the God of Abraham. "Clap your hands, all ye peoples; shout unto God with the voice of triumph. The princes of the peoples are gathered together, the people of the God of Abraham; for unto God belong the shields of the earth; He is greatly exalted" (Psalms 47 vv. 2, 10).

The Opposite of Abraham

Our present Torah portion continues the story of the life of Abraham, who was the epitome of faith in God, humility, charity and kindness. Woven in with this story and in counterpoint to it, a central part of our portion describes the overthrow of Sodom and its neighboring cities, which went to the opposite extreme in denial of God, arrogance, selfishness and cruelty. For "the men of Sodom were very wicked and sinful to God" (Gen. 13:13).

Prior to their overthrow, the Torah tells us that the surrounding Jordan plain was "like a garden of God" (Genesis 13:10) on account of its exceptional fertility and beauty. But the moral degeneracy of its inhabitants brought about their destruction through "fire and sulfur from heaven" (Gen. 19:24) - a cataclysmic ecological disaster that caused the loss of their entire culture forever, turning the surrounding area into a barren, arid, rocky desert inhospitable to vegetable or animal life, as can be seen until today in the aptly-named "Dead" Sea region of Israel and Jordan.

What was the sin of the men of Sodom?

While Abraham came to teach us to be kind to one another, the inhabitants of Sodom practiced the exact opposite. This can be seen in their attitude to the angels who came in human guise to visit

Abraham's nephew Lot: the inhabitants wanted to sexually rape them (Genesis 19:5). Nothing could be further from the hospitality to strangers practiced by Abraham as part of his kindness, as described in the preceding chapter, with which our portion opens (Genesis 18:1-16).

The people of Sodom were blessed with exceptional natural advantages yet refused to share them with anyone else. They strictly forbade and ruthlessly avenged any act of charity of kindness. The Torah sages told of one young girl who took pity on a starving wayfarer and fed him, for which she was punished by being coated with honey and left on a roof to the mercy of the wasps (Rashi on Genesis 18:21). In Sodom there was one legendary bed for all visitors: one who was too short was stretched to fit the bed while one who was too tall was cut down to the right size (Midrash). Such tales illustrate the total fixation of the Sodomites on their own selfish interests while being stone-heartedly indifferent to the needs, pain, and suffering and basic human dignity of anyone else. Until today those who insist on imposing their own cast-iron rules on others without the least sensitivity to their true needs and interests are guilty of the same.

Outwardly, the people of Sodom may have seemed highly sophisticated, which could have been one reason why Abraham's nephew Lot had chosen to dwell with them (Genesis 13:10-11). But when the two angels came to visit Lot in Sodom, the inhabitants quickly revealed their true nature when they demanded that Lot should bring them out so that they might "know" them (Genesis 19:5). This was a euphemistic way of saying they wanted to submit these visitors to a brutal, humiliating, homosexual anal rape.

This was in total defiance of the universal Noahide Torah code, in which the fourth of the Seven Laws strictly forbids such acts of sexual immorality since they degrade the human sexual function from being the foundation of marital love and human procreation into the sordid gratification of sheer physical lust.

God commanded man to "be fruitful and multiply" (Genesis 1:28), and implanted in him the very powerful sexual drive to ensure that men and women would instinctively seek each other out in order to bond and reproduce so as to ensure the future of the human race. Within the marital relationship, sexual intimacy is precious and holy, raising us above mere animalism and binding husband and wife together in the love that provides a nurturing environment for raising and educating children to follow the path of God.

The fourth of the Seven Commandments includes the following prohibitions (Rambam, Laws of Kings 9:5-8):

1. A man may not marry nor have relations with his biological mother. The same applies to his father's wife even if she is not his mother.

2. Maternal brothers and sisters are forbidden to marry one another.

3. A man may not have relations with another man's wife. Adultery is strictly prohibited because it undermines the sanctity of marriage, in which the bond between husband and wife is exclusive.

4. It is forbidden for humans to have relations with animals or birds of any kind ("bestiality").

5. It is forbidden for males, whether adults or minors, to practice anal sexual relations where the active partner plays a male role while the passive partner plays a female role ("sodomy").

Sodomy is ultimately degrading to both partners and is particularly abhorrent because the active partner ejaculates human seed - which has the power to create future generations made in God's image - into the anus, which is a place of stinking waste.

Immorality in the mass media

It would be appropriate for serious citizens who embrace the Seven Commandments to reflect on the lessons of the destruction of Sodom for contemporary society and culture, which are plagued with extreme moral laxity and blatant indecency, particularly in the mass media and popular entertainment. These have tremendous influence on people's attitudes and behavior, but in many countries, the last few decades have seen the abandonment of all restraint in what is shown in advertising, newspapers and magazines, on television, in movies and now on the Internet. One of the driving forces of this trend is the astronomical sums of money that are being made through the exploitation of the sexual drive.

At the click of a mouse, the Internet makes instantly available images and videos of every kind of overt sexual activity including those that are most abhorrent in the eyes of the Torah - sodomy, bestiality and the shameless spilling of seed. It appears that behind closed doors all over the world and sometimes even on the very streets and in open places, entire subcultures have grown up around these practices.

The consensus in many (though not all) parts of the world today is that consenting adults should be left free to practice what they want as long as they do not try to involve minors or other people against their will. Yet the rampant immodesty in the media encourages immoral behavior and is itself an invasion of the privacy of the many citizens who have no wish to be subject to this assault on their senses and those of their children.

One of the greatest challenges to those wishing to follow the Seven Commandments and teach them to their children is to protect them from the negative influence of the surrounding permissiveness. Parents who care for the long-term welfare of their children must make every effort to filter what their children are exposed to on

TV and other media, and make assiduous efforts to educate them in the Seven Commandments in order to immunize them as best as possible against this negative influence.

Even if society permits consenting adults to do what they please in private, this does not justify the blatant flaunting of that which is abhorrent to the Torah in public forums, on TV, the Internet and other media. It would be a great act of courage in the spirit of Abraham for Noahides to join together to protest this trend and instead promote the pathway that Abraham taught to his offspring.

"And Abraham will surely be a great and mighty nation, and all the nations of the earth will be blessed through him. For I know him, that he will instruct his children and household after him to guard the way of God to practice charity and justice, in order that God should bring upon Abraham what He has spoken about him" (Genesis 18:18-19).

Rites of Passage

The living and the dead

As Sarah's life in this world comes to an end, the Torah makes an exact reckoning of her years: "And the life of Sarah was one hundred and twenty-seven years: these were the years of the life of Sarah" (Gen. 23:1).

As we live our lives from moment to moment, day by day and year by year, our thoughts tend to be more focused on the present and the future, while most of what is past and gone is usually forgotten. Yet in fact every thought, word and deed of every moment are registered and recorded in God's "book" - His eternal memory, which is surely perfect. The Torah's careful accounting of the years of Sarah's life comes to teach us that when the soul leaves the body after death, all the person's days and years ascend together to be judged in the heavenly court in accordance with God's perfect justice. This is in order to determine that person's fitting place in the life after life. For "the righteous of the peoples of the world have a share in the world to come" (Maimonides, Laws of Repentance 3:5). Each one must surely be judged in order to attain his or her rightful share.

While the soul of the departed goes on to face what it must face in the heavenly court, the living must pay their last respects, accompanying the

40

dead person's earthly remains to their final resting place. The Torah sages call the accompaniment of the dead at their funeral "*true* kindness" because it is performed with complete altruism, since the living can expect nothing in return from the dead person.

Participation in a funeral is listed among the acts of kindness for which those who perform them gain their main reward in the World to Come while eating the "fruits" in this world (Pe'ah 1:1). Among these "fruits" are the deeper humility and wisdom we attain when face to face with the existential truth of human mortality at a funeral. The rites with which we mark a person's passage from this world to the next are as much for the benefit of the living as they are for the dead.

Thus, Abraham marked the death of his beloved wife with eulogies and mourning. "And Sarah died in Kiryat Arba, which is Hebron, in the land of Canaan, and Abraham came to eulogize Sarah and to weep for her" (Genesis 23:2). Recalling the fine points of the departed and mourning their loss increases our appreciation of the preciousness of life and the importance of using each moment for the greatest possible good.

Rites of passage

The stories in the book of Genesis include a number of references to various rites of passage. In the previous portion, **Vayeira**, we read of the feast made by Abraham to mark his son Isaac's transition from early childhood dependence upon motherly care and attention to the expanded horizons of flourishing boyhood. "And the child grew and was weaned, and Abraham made a great *feast* on the day of the weaning of Isaac" (Genesis 21:8). The Torah commentators teach us that it was called a "*great* feast" not because of lavish catering and gushing wine but "because the *great* people of the generation were there: Shem, Eiver and Avimelech" (see Rashi ad loc.). In inviting wise sages and leaders, Abraham surely wanted to use this auspicious occasion in Isaac's life to impress upon him the serious responsibility that falls upon the mature individual to order all his or her affairs and dealings in this world with wisdom.

Marriage

Our present portion deals not only with the rites of passage with which we attend the dead but also with the subject of pairing and marriage, which are the necessary foundation for breeding and raising new generations. Finding a suitable marriage partner is the main theme of Genesis chapter 24, one of the lengthier chapters in the Bible. Now that Isaac has attained full adulthood, his father Abraham sees that he is ripe for marriage. With Sarah no longer here to look for a suitable partner, Abraham sends his faithful servant Eliezer to search in the land from which he came, where his family still reside.

The actual rites of passage for bride and groom as they move from single to married life are mentioned later in Genesis. To celebrate Jacob's wedding with his daughter, Laban "gathered all the people of the place and made a feast" (Genesis 29:22). In that same passage we learn that the wedding festivities lasted seven days (ibid. verse 27).

A public marriage ceremony with a celebrant, witnesses and other participants is important under the Seven Noahide Laws, which strictly forbid adultery. The couple's change in status from being unattached to being man and wife is a serious matter that must be made evident to all in order to protect the sanctity of their marriage from destructive extra-marital affairs.

For the couple themselves, the wedding celebrations with dear ones and friends are and should be a glorious send-off on their new life together. But the future of the marriage will not be assured simply by holding a riotous party with lots of booze, noise and fun. The groundwork for marriage must be carefully laid in advance of the ceremony by choosing the right partner. That is why the Torah focuses less on the marital rite of passage - Jacob's wedding party is described in one verse (Genesis 29:22) - but much more on how Eliezer set about finding a suitable life-partner for Isaac, where the narrative consists of sixty-seven verses.

Isaac's marriage to Rebecca was not merely an "arranged-marriage" in the sense that they were forced upon one another by their respective families. Rebecca's right to choose her own husband was strictly respected by her family. "And they said, 'Let us call the girl and ask her directly'. They called Rebecca and said to her, 'Will you go with this man?' And she said, 'I will go'" (Genesis 29:57-8).

Nevertheless, Rebecca's marriage with Isaac was "arranged" in the sense that Eliezer was cast in the role of the matchmaker charged with finding a suitable candidate to be the wife of his master's beloved son, who would in due course succeed Abraham in leading the world in the service of God.

Rebecca was indeed "of very good appearance" (verse 16), which is an excellent recommendation for any potential bride. But it was not primarily for her beauty that Eliezer chose her, because even before he had even seen her he had already devised a test by which to assess the character of potential candidates. The right one would be the girl who would not only give him to drink as he stood at the well late in the day after a grueling ride through the desert, but would also offer to water his ten camels (verse 14). This manifestation of exceptional kindness going well beyond the strict "letter of the law" would mark her out as a fitting wife for Isaac and a fitting daughter-in-law of Abraham, the outstanding exemplar of human kindness. When choosing a marriage partner one should go not merely by external appearance but by true character.

The Birthday Party

Another important point of transition in our lives is the yearly anniversary of our day of birth. In most years, our birthdays mark less of a transition in our lives than major transitions such as from childhood or adolescence to maturity and adulthood or from single to married life. Even so, the day on which we start a new year in our allotted span of life is still a milestone that may properly be marked with an appropriate celebration.

Thus, we find that in the time of Joseph, Pharaoh marked his birthday by reinstating his butler (who according to tradition had been imprisoned for letting a fly get into the king's wine), while executing his baker (who had nearly killed him by letting a stone get into his bread, see Genesis 40:20 and Rashi ad loc.). Pharaoh did not merely hold a loud birthday party. He evidently used the occasion of his birthday to review and settle affairs of state.

Each of us is king or queen in his or her own life and it is likewise proper for us to celebrate the anniversary of our birthday in a fitting manner with dear ones and friends. A feast with good food and drink is an appropriate time to bless, praise and thank God for the sum of years He has given us so far. We should also reflect on the preciousness of life and our true purpose in this world, and pray to God to use the time He gives us to attain it.

"So, teach us to number our days, that we may get a heart of wisdom" (Psalms 90:12). By remembering God and turning to Him at important moments of transition in our own lives and the lives of our dear ones and friends, we elevate our days and years, so that when our time comes to leave this world they will all rise before the heavenly court to testify in our favor.

TOLDOT Genesis 25:19-28:9

Who is Strong?

Following the passing of Abraham, Isaac moves to the center of the stage in our present portion. While Abraham is the exemplar of the expansive quality of Kindness (Hebrew: *Chessed*), Isaac is the exemplar of the opposite pole: Strength (Hebrew: *Gevurah*). This includes such important traits as the ability to focus and apply one's personal powers constructively through self-control, restraint and discipline. As such, the quality of Strength is the necessary complement to the quality of Kindness, which must be carefully focused in order to attain its true goal.

Isaac manifested the quality of Strength when he submitted to Abraham's binding him for sacrifice on the altar of the service of God (Genesis chapter 22). Abraham's quality of Kindness and Isaac's quality of Strength then became synthesized in the personality of Isaac's son Jacob, who also makes his first appearance in our present portion. The biblical text later describes Jacob as "perfect" (Genesis 33:18) in virtue of his ability to attain balance in the application of these two qualities.

The Godly and the Animal Soul: the higher and lower selves

"Who is called strong? The person who controls his inclination" (Avot 4:1). According to Torah psychology, God has created us with two sides: a good inclination (rooted in the "Godly Soul" or "higher self") and an evil inclination (rooted in the "Animal Soul" or "lower self"). These two sides are given to test us. We constantly face all kinds of choices in life, and often we are pulled in different directions by conflicting inner forces. One side - the good inclination - leans toward the "straight and narrow path" of virtue, but the other side - the evil inclination - pulls in the opposite direction. The choices we make determine our destiny both in this world and in the life after life in the world to come.

The good inclination is characterized by selflessness in devotion to G-d, benefiting other people and cultivation of the higher self or soul. The evil inclination prompts us to serve ourselves and our mundane cravings and desires, whether for food and drink, sex and other physical pleasures or for wealth, power, prestige, honor and the like. The path to God is through binding ourselves on the altar of God's service and sacrificing the lower self through submission to His will as revealed in the Torah. This requires self-control.

Money and Charity

We cannot survive in this world without eating and drinking, cohabitation and a host of other material requirements. God does not demand that we remove ourselves completely from the material world, but rather that we satisfy our legitimate needs honestly without taking more than we need. In the modern economy everyone needs money to buy what they need, but often because of fear that they may lack money at some future time, many people throw themselves into the frantic race to acquire more and more wealth in the hope of providing themselves with "security" and enjoying a higher standard of living.

One of our greatest tests in the struggle between the good and bad inclinations is how we go about making our living, and what we do with our wealth and money. Do we keep it all to ourselves, or do we share some of it with others?

Tithes

The economy of the Biblical world did involve money (as when Abraham purchased a burial cave for Sarah with "ready cash" - four hundred shekel-weights of silver (Genesis 23:16). However, the Biblical economy was primarily based upon agriculture, and Isaac's way of going about the cultivation of his field teaches us an important lesson about how to make our livelihood in an honest, God-fearing way.

"And Isaac sowed in that land, and in that year he found *one hundred measures*. And God blessed him, and the man grew and went on growing until he was very great" (Genesis 26:12-13). The second verse quoted here is telling us that through God's blessing Isaac became very prosperous, while the first verse hints to us as to the particular merit displayed by Isaac that brought forth this blessing.

How did Isaac become so rich? The Torah commentators tell us that even before he sowed his field, Isaac estimated how much such a field should produce, but when he finally harvested the crop he found it to be one hundred times greater than his original estimate! But why did Isaac want to estimate the likely yield even before he sowed? The commentators say that he wanted to assess the amount of the tithe he would give to the poor from his eventual harvest (Rashi ad loc.).

We may thus infer that the reason why God blessed Isaac with his great wealth was because of his good intention. Even before he started sowing his field, he was already thinking about giving a portion of the eventual yield to the needy. In an agricultural society you have to farm in order to eat. But Isaac thought not only about providing his own needs but also about satisfying the needs of others through giving tithes.

The first appearance in the Torah of the concept of giving tithes is when Abraham gave a tenth of the booty he took in his war against the Four Kings to

Malki-Tzedek (Genesis 14:20). Malki-Tzedek was a priest, and it is a Torah principle that those who minister to G-d should have their material needs satisfied through the tithes they receive from the rest of the people (cf. Genesis 47:22). This way they are able to devote themselves entirely to their vocation without having to divert their attention to physical labor. The Torah elaborates a complete system of tithes (Terumot and Maasrot) which the Israelite farmer must give to the Temple priests (Cohanim), to the Levites, who ministered as the Temple guards and singers, and to the poor (see Numbers chapter 18; Deuteronomy 14:28).

Charity

These tithes are to be separated from agricultural produce. However, not everyone is a farmer. For those whose livelihood comes to them not in the form of the crops they harvest but through their paycheck or other earnings, the monetary equivalent of the agricultural tithe is charity (Hebrew: *Tzedakah*). While even a small gift of money to a needy person is considered charity, the Torah guideline for tithing one's income is that where possible, one should give at least one tenth and preferably one fifth of one's net earnings to charity.

Giving a portion of one's income to charity is a Torah commandment: "If there be among you a needy man... you shall not harden your heart or shut your hand from your needy brother but you shall surely open your hand to him" (Deuteronomy 15:7-8); "And if your brother is poor and his means fail with you, then you shall support him; whether he is a stranger or a settler, he shall live with you" (Leviticus 25:35). The Torah commandment to give charity applies not only to the Israelites but to all the nations. Thus it is written that Abraham taught his offspring that "they shall guard the way of God to practice *charity* and justice" (Genesis 18:19; Rabbeinu Nissim of Gerona on Sanhedrin 56b).

God is perfect goodness, and it is in the nature of goodness to do good for the benefit of others. Through the practice of charity we learn to set a limit to our selfish enjoyment of our own wealth by giving a portion of it to other people who are in need. This way we may inculcate something of God's perfect altruism in our own hearts.

Many people are forced to become slaves in all but name in order to earn their livelihood, and many are slaves to their money and possessions. The way to free ourselves from this enslavement to money is by thinking of others too. We are not commanded to give away everything we earn to charity, for then we ourselves would fall into dependency upon others for our livelihood. What we have to give is a "tithe" - a proportion - of our earnings. After having done so, we ourselves are entitled to enjoy the fruits of our labors.

We should carefully choose the recipients of our charity in order to avoid giving away our money to the unscrupulous. But sometimes it is hard to determine whether a potential recipient is truly worthy or not. In such cases it may be preferable to help them anyway in case they really are worthy rather than risk turning away those who are genuinely needy just because some beggars may be fakers. The purpose of charity is not only to satisfy people's physical needs for food and drink, clothing, housing and the like, but also to satisfy the spiritual needs of hungry souls through supporting the study and teaching of the Torah.

When we are confronted with a needy person stretching out his hand for help, the evil inclination often reacts with stonehearted indifference and even cruelty, saying: "Why should I give my precious, hard-earned money to this offensive individual?" We have to break this instinctive selfishness and force ourselves to open our hearts and our hands: "You shall surely open your hand." Those who force themselves to do this are truly strong.

The Work Ethic

As an old man, Jacob said to Pharaoh: "Little and evil were the days of the years of my life" (Genesis 47:9). Our present portion depicts the struggles of Jacob in his earlier years, as he flees from the wrath of his brother Esau to take refuge with his duplicitous uncle Laban, against whose wiles he struggles for years in order to marry, build his family and establish himself as a man of substance in the world.

After twenty years with Laban, Jacob "increased exceedingly, and had large flocks and maid-servants and men-servants and camels and asses" (Genesis 30:43). All Jacob's wealth and even his very wives were gained through hard work and effort, as he himself testified to Laban when the latter tried to swindle him out of his just rewards:

"It is now twenty years that I have been with you. Your sheep and your goats did not cast their young, and I did not eat the rams of your flock. I did not bring you an animal that was preyed upon; I bore the loss. From my hand you required it, whether stolen by day or stolen by night. By day the drought consumed me and the ice by night, and sleep fled from my eyes. This is now twenty years that I have been in your house. I worked for you for fourteen years for your daughters and six years for your flock, and you have changed my wages ten times" (Genesis 31:38-41).

Although Laban repeatedly deceived Jacob, the latter refused to take any kind of vengeance or permit himself to deal with him dishonestly. This was because Jacob wanted nothing from this world that he had not earned through honest work and effort. He did not want to eat "the bread of shame" that a person receives as a free, unearned and undeserved gift from someone else.

The nobility of work

Working for one's just deserts is a fundamental pillar of the Torah outlook. God's purpose in creation was to give His creatures a share of His own perfect goodness, but "God's wisdom decreed that for such good to be perfect, the one enjoying it must be its master. He must be one who has earned it for himself, and not one given it accidentally or by chance. God therefore decreed and arranged that creation contain elements of both perfection and deficiency, as well as a creature [man] with equal access to both. This creature would then be given the means to both acquire perfection and avoid deficiency...The more elements of perfection this creature incorporates into itself, the stronger will be his association and bond to God, deriving both pleasure and perfection from His goodness, while he is himself the master of this good and perfection, having acquired them by choosing them" (Rabbi Moshe Hayim Luzzatto,

"The Way of God", translated by Rabbi Aryeh Kaplan, Feldheim Publishers, pp. 39-41).

One of the ways God has given mankind to purify and refine both ourselves and the world is through working to make a living. God created the world incomplete - with endless potential yet a multitude of deficiencies - so that the creatures themselves would have to *act* and *do*, as written at the conclusion of the account of creation: "which He created *to do* " (Genesis 2:3:). Thus, wheat cannot be plucked from the stalk and eaten immediately but must be processed, hulled, ground, combined with other ingredients and baked or cooked to provide tasty food, etc.

If people stopped working, the world would go to ruin. But "...not for devastation did He create it; He fashioned it for a habitation" (Isaiah 45:18). God desires a civilized, developed world in which we constantly improve the way we utilize its amazing resources to provide the best possible life for all its inhabitants, materially and spiritually. God desires that we should earn our living with dignity through work and effort, and not depend upon others except in cases of genuine need.

Prohibition of Theft

One of the Seven Noahide commandments that apply to all mankind is not to take what one wants or needs from others without their consent - through robbery or theft.

Robbery is when one takes or snatches something from another blatantly and shamelessly (cf. II Samuel 23:21). Theft and stealing are carried out in such a way that the person who suffers the loss is not aware of it at the time.

Robbery and theft occur not only in the lawless world of criminal thieves and robbers, but in all kinds of subtler forms "in broad daylight", not only on the street or in the marketplace but also when powerful monopolies, consortiums, vested interests and governments corner large sections of the populace into having to accept low wages while paying extortionate prices and taxes, helping further line the pockets of the rich. Many highly-placed officials receive bribes and other benefits to give away money and resources that do not belong to them, magnifying their own expense claims etc., literally stealing from the public chest.

In our present Torah portion, Jacob - alone and without support - deals with one of the most ingenious thieves and exploiters of all times, the wily Laban, yet does not permit himself to take vengeance and steal anything back. This comes to teach that even when faced with surrounding malpractice and corruption, the God-fearing citizen of the world does not allow him or herself to fall to the same low level, knowing that we are commanded not to steal.

Avoid stealing

While theft is often a matter of stealing actual goods or money, there are many other ways in which people wittingly or unthinkingly steal from others. To avoid willful or unintentional theft:

- Traders must practice honesty in accurately weighing and measuring their wares and asking a fair price for a fair deal, without deceiving or overcharging the buyer.
- Employers may not exploit workers but must pay a fair wage that must be given on time.
- The employee is obliged to work diligently without taking unnecessary rest periods, a drink here and a snack there, attending to personal phone calls and emails during work hours, etc. Stealing from the time one owes to the employer in return for one's wages is also a form of theft.

Rest vs. Laziness

No-one should have to work all the time. Rest, relaxation, recreation and appropriate entertainment are perfectly right and legitimate as they give us the strength to accomplish our work and our mission in this world. Inactivity leads to boredom, which can cause a host of evils. The Torah teaches us the value of work - for each one in his or her pathway and vocation. In the words of Shimon the Righteous (High Priest in Jerusalem in the time of Alexander the Great): "The world stands upon three things: on the Torah, on *work* and on acts of kindness" (Avot 1:2). He was referring to the holy work of the Temple priests, to our daily work and service of prayer, and to actual mundane, everyday work.

"One that is slack in his work is brother to the destroyer" (Proverbs 18:9).

"Go to the ant, you lazy one; consider her ways, and be wise. She has no chief, overseer or ruler, but she provides her bread in the summer and gathers her food in the harvest. How long will you sleep, O lazy one? When will you get up out of your sleep? 'Just a little sleep, a little slumber, a little folding of hands to sleep' - so shall your poverty come as a runner and your need and lack as an armed man." (Proverbs 6:6-11).

Rape!!!

Our portion continues the story of the life of Jacob following his return to the Promised Land after his twenty-year sojourn in Haran to escape the wrath of his twin brother Esau. Now a wealthy man with wives, children and livestock, Jacob must first pacify Esau in order to be able to settle peaceably in the Land. A potentially devastating encounter ends with their agreement to coexist (Genesis 22:3-33:16), and Jacob advances into the Promised Land and sets up camp outside the city of Shechem (Genesis 33:17-18).

Jacob did not seek free residency. Just as his grandfather Abraham had purchased Promised Land real estate - the Cave of Makhpelah - for ready cash, so Jacob paid one hundred talents to buy the field where he encamped from its Canaanite owners, the sons of Hamor the Hivite, prince of the land, among whom the most noteworthy was Shechem (ibid. 33:19, 34:19). Jacob then built an Altar to call upon his Maker and affirm His kingship over him.

It was only natural that Jacob's young daughter Dinah would want to go out and explore her new neighborhood and see if she could find some friends among the local girls. As soon as she did so, the glamorous Prince Shechem, having just concluded a lucrative property sale with her father, saw her, fancied her, kidnapped and raped her (ibid. 34:1-2).

Kidnap and rape under Torah law

The Torah views the kidnap of a person as the most serious form of theft. It is strictly prohibited on pain of death under the Noahide code and in the eighth of the Ten Commandments (Maimonides, Laws of Theft 9:1-6; Exodus 20:13 and Rashi ad loc.).

The Torah also abhors rape, which is explicitly equated with murder (Deuteronomy 22:25-7). To gratify his own animal lust, the rapist seizes and humiliates the victim against her will, robbing her of her innocence and leaving her marked for life physically, emotionally and spiritually. This is a terrible offence against the dignity of woman. It is also a brutal violation of the Torah moral code, which sets the highest value upon the sanctity and purity of the marital relationship as the foundation for rearing healthy future citizens of the world. It is a girl's fundamental right to choose her partner in life and to come to her marriage as a virgin. The Torah does not favor casual sexual encounters between unattached singles and certainly abhors rape.

The treatment of Dinah was viewed as a grave offense by her brothers, the sons of Jacob: "And the sons of Jacob came in from the field when they heard it; and the men were grieved, and they were very angry, because he had done a vile deed in

Israel in lying with Jacob's daughter - a thing that ought not to be done" (Genesis 34:7).

Under Torah law a raped woman is not obliged to marry her rapist (Maimonides, Laws of the Virgin Maiden 1:3). But while continuing to hold Dinah captive, Shechem sought to give legitimacy to their relationship by prompting his father to negotiate a marriage agreement with her family. Hamor's proposed agreement made future peaceful coexistence, intermarriage and commerce between the Canaanites and Jacob's family contingent upon their agreement to Dinah's marriage with Shechem.

The sons of Jacob craftily stipulated that the men of Shechem would have to be circumcised, to which they agreed. But while they were in great physical pain after the painful surgical operation, two of Dinah's brothers - Simon and Levy, who were still no more than teenagers - entered the town and put all the men to the sword and plundered everything else (Genesis 34:8-29).

Was this just?

From the point of view of Noahide law, Shechem and his conniving father Hamor were liable to the death penalty for perpetrating kidnap and rape (Maimonides, Laws of Theft loc. cit., Laws of Kings 9:9). The men of the town with whom Hamor and Shechem came to talk "at the gate of their city" (Genesis 34:20) were the town residents. The "gate" was where they met together in council.

Under the seventh of the Universal Noahide Commandments, they were obliged to establish a court of law to duly punish Shechem and Hamor. Instead, they aided and abetted them.

Since they were the rulers of the land, there was no-one else to impose justice. Thus, Simon and Levy - two teenagers - had no option but to take the law into their own hands, using cunning to overcome the numerical advantage of the wrongdoers in order to carry out their lawful execution.

Jacob criticized Simon and Levy not because he considered their action morally wrong but because he feared that it was strategically dangerous: "And Jacob said to Simon and Levy: 'You have troubled me, to make me odious to the inhabitants of the land, the Canaanites and the Perizzites; and, I being few in number, they will gather themselves together against me and strike me; and I shall be destroyed, I and my house.'" (verse 30).

But Simon and Levy justly answer back: "Should our sister be treated as a harlot?" (verse 31). To this Jacob gave no answer.

Some questions for today

The biblical tale of the rape of a young girl by a powerful despot rings with special poignancy today not only because sexual promiscuity and actual rape are so very rampant in our societies but also because the very minds and souls of our young people are "raped" from the earliest ages through the licentiousness that is all around us and that invades us in the privacy of our very homes through the power of contemporary communications media.

Today's older generation remember that until the 1960's a certain standard of modesty prevailed in public forums, in the press, TV and radio, enter-tainment, advertising, etc. However, this subse-quently came under attack as being "repressive" and "unhealthy", and through the influence of some leading "thinkers" and "philosophers" together with growing numbers of "artists", "entertainers" and "celebrities", the flood-gates were opened to the new culture of freedom, liberation and moral license that now prevails.

Today sex education is considered a vital part of school curriculums for pre-teens. Little children - like everyone else - are exposed to all kinds of TV, movie, press and advertising images that are unfit even for mature adults. Popular music and movies are constantly suggestive if not downright explicit. Through the revolution in communications tech-nology, every kind of pictures, videos, instant mes-saging, phone-chat and much more are available to 9 and 10-year olds, while the entire underbelly of worldwide sexual excess is accessible via the Internet on the click of a mouse.

What can we do?

Those seeking to lead their lives in accordance with the Torah code of modesty may feel they have little or no power to influence the surrounding permissive culture. One challenge is to filter what comes into the home and the mind through the TV, Internet, cell phones, newspapers, magazines etc. when these are now essential parts of people's lives. How can parents and educators fight the rape of children's minds through inappropriate images and other pernicious influences? Tragically, the damage is all too often already done by the time the parent recognizes it, when filtering is no longer a possibility.

Parents should shed tears in prayer to God that their children should grow and mature in purity, find their true soul mate and establish a home based on God's laws and teachings. We should pray for compassion on those who are far from this path. Wherever possible, parents should seek to protect their children from exposure to harmful surrounding influences, striving to build their immunity through exemplary behavior and coherent explanation of the Torah principles of moral purity, which correspond to what wisdom and good sense dictate. It would be desirable to establish friendship circles and support networks with like-minded people. The most effective protest against present-day indecency will be for God-fearing citizens of the world to join together to promote

TORAH FOR THE NATIONS

the proper education of our children in true Torah standards of dignity and morality.

How Can Brothers Get Along?

Our present portion and the three portions that follow it until the conclusion of the book of Genesis tell the dramatic story of the feud between Joseph and his brothers with its many twists and turns until it is finally resolved.

The story of this feud between brothers and its eventual resolution is of deep significance to all mankind since we are all brothers and sisters, children of Noah and descendants of his three sons, Shem Ham and Japheth. We surely yearn for peace, yet almost all human history has been wracked by prolonged feuds between and within peoples, nations, clans and families... Yet God's plan is for all humanity to unite "with one accord" [Hebrew: **shechem**] in the service of the One God (Zephaniah 3:9). A study of strife among brothers in the Torah may offer clues to how the unification of our hearts might be possible.

Brotherly strife in the Torah

The first two brothers in the world, Cain and Abel, struggled with one another for world dominion. Cain was the older of the two, yet God favored Abel, arousing Cain's envy and hatred to the point where he shed his own brother's blood (Genesis 4:3-8). We see that hatred is rooted in jealousy and can lead to literal murder.

Noah's sons were a trio - Shem, Ham and Japheth. After the flood, when Noah planted a vineyard and became drunk, Ham showed himself the "bad apple" when he his father's nakedness and went and publicized the fact to his brothers. Yet this lowly behavior evoked a beautiful display of brotherly cooperation by Shem and Japheth, who walked backwards into Noah's tent with a garment on their shoulders [Hebrew: **shechem**] to cover him, modestly averting their faces so as not to see him in his degradation (Gen. 9:23).

Noah cursed Ham's offspring to be "servant of servants" to their brothers, while he blessed Shem and Japheth with the blessing of brotherly cooperation: "God will make Japheth beautiful and he will dwell in the tents of Shem" (Genesis 9:27). Humanity needs wise leadership, and those who are truly fit to give this must hold sway while all the rest of the people must defer to them. Japheth was in fact Noah's firstborn (Rashi on Genesis 10:21), yet he was to seek spiritual leadership "in the tents" of his younger brother, Shem.

Thus, it was the offspring of Abraham the "Shem-ite", or Semite, who inherited the mission of giving spiritual leadership to the whole world. Yet even among those offspring, feuds between brothers started immediately when Ishmael rose up against Isaac (Genesis 21:9). Ishmael was firstborn to his mother Hagar and thirteen years older than Isaac, who was Sarah's firstborn. Under the Torah law of inheritance, it is the firstborn of a man's *first* wife, even if she is hated, who receives the firstborn's double portion of his estate (Deut. 21:16-17). Yet God Himself said that Abraham's line would pass through Isaac (Gen. 21:12).

Isaac's sons Esau and Jacob were twins from the same mother. Esau came first out of the womb, yet the birthright and the blessings were acquired by "little" Jacob, later named Israel, whom God chose as His firstborn (Exodus 4:22). There are numerous other cases in the Bible where a younger brother is given prominence, as when Jacob gave seniority to Ephraim over Joseph's firstborn Manasseh (Genesis 48:14) and when God chose Moses over his older brother Aaron (as discussed below) and chose David, the messianic king and redeemer, over all of his older brothers (I Samuel 16:11).

What made Joseph's brother's hate him?

Jacob's first love had been Rachel, but she gave birth to her own firstborn Joseph only after Jacob already had ten sons, six from his first wife, Leah and another four from the handmaidens Bilhah and Zilpah. The birthright should have gone to Leah's firstborn Reuben but was taken from him for wrongdoing (Genesis 35:22). Leah's next two sons, Shimon and Levy, had invoked Jacob's wrath for their sack of the city of Shechem (Genesis 34:30), so next in line stood Judah, from whom in fact the royal line of David went forth (Genesis 38:29 and 49:8-12; Ruth 4:18-22).

The argument over who should hold sway over the Children of Israel was essentially between Joseph (Rachel's firstborn) and Judah (Leah's fourth son; see Genesis 44:18). Joseph's older brothers were already jealous of him because of the favoritism showed him by Jacob: it is natural in families that when a new baby arrives and seemingly receives all the love and attention, the supplanted older siblings can become very jealous, spiteful and vengeful.

When Joseph told his brothers his first dream about the sheaves of corn, they asked him in shock: "Will you surely rule over us, will you surely govern us?" (Genesis 36:8). The idea that their spoiled little brother would be king over them made them hate him even more. People who are filled with feelings of their own importance detest the very thought of being subordinate to those they despise. Joseph's brother's hatred made them want to purge him from the world, but a measure of brotherly instinct prevailed when instead they sold him into exile and slavery (37:26-27).

It is in the ensuing Torah portions that the gripping story unfolds of how Joseph attains greatness in Egypt and eventually uses his consummate skill and wisdom to manipulate his brothers into seeing the evil of their deed until they repent completely. In the end Jacob gave Joseph one extra "portion" over his brothers (Gen. 48:22; Hebrew: **shechem**). The final resolution of their feud comes only in the closing chapter of Genesis (50:15ff). The story indeed continues to unfold until today, because the Ten Lost Tribes under the leadership of Ephraim have still not been reconciled with the Jewish People under the leadership of Judah and the House of David (see Ezekiel 37:16-28).

Humility

The most perfect Biblical story of brotherly love and cooperation is that of Moses and Aaron. Again, Aaron was the older of the two brothers, yet when God chose Moses for the mission of redeeming Israel from their exile, Aaron rejoiced (Exodus 4:14).

Moses became the Law-Giver (teacher of Torah, God's revelation to us) while Aaron became the Priest (Temple service, prayer). Each of the two brothers knew their own role and mission and had no envy for the other. Moses and Aaron - the teacher and the priest - were perfect examples of humility, mutual respect and love. Each was what he was while deferring to the other in the other's unique sphere.

People wage wars against one another because they do not want to be subordinate to those whom they perceive as being unworthy of holding sway. Indeed, in today's world many of the rulers, legislators and judges etc. are obviously quite corrupt and unworthy. Yet throughout history it has been seen that those who are truly worthy to rule have at first been oppressed and persecuted. This in itself engenders humility in the true ruler, but the people too must have the humility to recognize when their perceptions have been in error so as to submit themselves to the true ruler. The demonized Joseph as he appeared in the eyes of his brothers may indeed have been a detestable figure, but this was not the true Joseph. That was what the brothers had to come to understand.

"How good and how pleasant it is for brothers to dwell in unity. It is like the precious oil upon the head, coming down upon the beard, even Aaron's beard..." (Psalms 133:1-2).

How to Avoid Catastrophe

"And it was at the end of two years, when Pharaoh was dreaming, and there he was standing over the river."

"At the *end* of two years": Joseph's rise to power was not immediate. It was destined to occur only at the *end* of a specific period, during which he continued to suffer in the pit. Thus, from the very beginning of our portion, we are directed to keep our eyes focused on the end, the future goal. Joseph's winning interpretation of Pharaoh's dreams of seven good cows and seven good ears of corn consumed in each case by seven bad ones is also focused on the end, the future, the time when we will have to face the consequences of our deeds today: Seven years of plenty are coming but they will be followed by seven years of famine. Don't squander the years of plenty, thinking only of present enjoyment. Look ahead, plan and act now so as to prepare for the years of dire hardship that are to come!

A universal lesson

"And Pharaoh said to his servants: Could there be found such a man that has the spirit of God in him? And Pharaoh said to Joseph: After God has made known to you all this, no-one is as understanding and wise as you" (Genesis 41:38-9). Pharaoh immediately appointed Joseph over his own household and over the whole of Egypt, then leader of the world in religion, wisdom, agriculture, engineering, architecture art and much else. Pharaoh's dream was not that of a mere private citizen but that of the king, having implications for the whole country and the whole world. This is what gives this story and Joseph's brilliant counsel, delivered in the presence of all Egypt's sages and counselors, universal importance in our times: Consume sparingly in good times in order to conserve for an unknown future. Joseph's plan, stated with such exquisite simplicity, clarity and beauty in our portion, is a lesson that all humanity, particularly our leaders, must truly and honestly take to heart.

Looming global catastrophe

I write these words towards the end of the first decade of the 21st century on December 18th 2009, just as leaders of 192 nations are gathered in Copenhagen, Denmark for a global summit on "Global Warming".

It takes little intelligence to understand that the global environment is rapidly changing with the most alarming present and likely future conse-quences in response to the huge amounts of emissions and other pollutants from all of the busy activities of earth's burgeoning human population as they go about the pursuit of ever higher standards of living with more cars, more jets, more gadgets and more of everything else for more and more people. This very pursuit is causing irreparable damage to the environment through wanton abuse of resources, horrifying pollution, deforestation and other evils often perpetrated by giant consortiums and vested financial interests with the complicity of top government officials. This is a global insanity that will lead inescapably to the decline and fall of human civilization as we know it.

Ironically the delegates in Copenhagen include prominent celebrities who have been most outspoken about the dangers of global warming and other threats while simultaneously maintaining their own fleets of private jets, flashy cars and energy-guzzling luxury estates. In fact, the entire summit is a hugely expensive and wasteful affair involving tens of thousands of personnel for what can only be described a crushingly disappointing result:

As reported by the world news media, the global "deal" addressing climate change includes pledges by developed countries to cut damaging emissions that **fall short of the minimum target** set by the United Nations Intergovernmental Panel on Climate Change. In other words, the leaders of the developed countries ignore their own advisors. It is reported that United States is willing to contribute $100 billion to a climate protection fund to make up for not improving on the recently announced emissions target. In other words, the United States is willing to pay a huge sum of money to avoid having to lose what they fear will be even more money if damaging emissions are reduced to recommended levels! It is reported that rich countries are ready to accept the principle that poor countries should not be legally bound to deliver on their commitments to reduce the rate of growth of their emissions - again, because this allows the rich countries not to deliver on their commitments either.

Mashiach

Who will bring these world leaders to their senses and persuade them to take the required steps to tackle the dire threats facing us instead of wheeler-dealing with each other to avoid doing what is necessary to save us from catastrophe?

It took God's intervention in Egypt by sending Pharaoh his dreams in order to bring Joseph to greatness as the wise counselor who saved Egypt and the then known world from disaster. Likewise, we today are looking to "the end", awaiting the shoot from the stock of Jesse upon whom the spirit of God shall rest, "the spirit of wisdom and understanding, the spirit of counsel and might, the spirit of knowledge and the fear of God. With righteousness shall he judge the poor and decide with equity for the meek of the land, and he shall smite the land with the rod of his mouth and with the breath of his lips shall he slay the wicked. And righteousness shall be the girdle of his loins and faithfulness the girdle of his reins." (Isaiah 11: 2-5).

Learning to say 'I was wrong'

Only one with a heart of stone could fail to be moved by the drama of Joseph's reconciliation with his brothers and his reunion with his father after having been given up for dead for 22 years.

Our present portion brings us to the very climax of the story, which takes up all of the last four out of the twelve portions of the book of Genesis, i.e. one third of the whole book. As discussed in the commentary on *Vayeishev (Genesis 37:1-40:23)*, conflict between brothers is also a recurrent theme throughout the earlier portions of Genesis (as in the case of Cain and Abel, the sons of Noah, Abraham and Lot, Isaac and Ishmael and Jacob and Esau). It is the fact that the conflict between Joseph and his brothers was eventually resolved peaceably that makes the lessons of this story so important for all humanity in our time, since the central issue we face is how we can all co-exist peacefully on this ever more crowded earth.

It is enough to take a glance at the news media to see how humanity is wracked with conflicts between opposing beliefs, cultures, blocs and nations as well as between different factions within countries, communities, work places and in people's very homes. Everyone believes that right and justice are on their side while their opponents are in the wrong. Few have the magnanimity to recognize that their enemies might also have a case, and people remain locked in self-protective and aggressive postures causing the cycle of conflict to continue.

It is not always true that both sides in a dispute must have a just case and that the dispute can be settled with a 50-50 compromise (cf. I Kings 3:16-28). God has made people with many different traits and temperaments; some have a tendency to greater placidity; others are more assertive. It is not uncommon for people to commit acts that encroach upon the lives of others, drawing them into conflict mode.

Joseph was not to blame for being Jacob's youngest son and the object of his favoritism, which made his brothers resentful. Undoubtedly Joseph's possibly well-intentioned reports to Jacob on their behavior only stoked the flames, as did his innocent telling of his dreams. His brothers became convinced that he was a terrible demon for whose extermination justice itself cried out. They all but killed him, selling him into the pain and degradation of slavery (Genesis ch. 37, see Rashi on v. 17).

Thus, we have in this story one victim and a gang of aggressors with murderous intentions. Yet in the end, after all the pain and anguish, the aggressors relent and the victim forgives.

It was Joseph who suffered the most (except for his father Jacob), yet Joseph's very suffering and subsequent ascent to his destined greatness taught him that "God kills and gives life, lowers people down to hell and brings them up" (I Samuel 2:6). For "happy is the man that God chastises and thereby You teach him from Your Torah" (Psalms 94:12). Joseph knew that even though his brothers had indeed sold him into slavery in Egypt, they were but agents of God, Who sent him ahead of them in order to provide for them and sustain them in their destined sojourn in that country.

It was Joseph's complete faith in God that enabled him to forgive his brothers for their crime against him and to display the noble magnanimity exemplified in his behavior throughout the story. As the forgiving victim, Joseph shows that he was firm in two of the fundamental pillars of faith:

1. God controls everything: Everything in the entire universe is under God's control. This includes everything that happens to you personally, both spiritually and materially, including what you yourself do, whether deliberately or unwittingly, willfully or under compulsion: everything is from God. Even when appearances suggest otherwise, the believer pays attention not to the external appearance of this world but to the underlying truth.

2. Reverses: When things appear to turn out badly for us, we have to accept that this is God's will and that whatever happens is for the best. Even when things go wrong because of something we ourselves may have thought, said or done, we must accept that this too is from God. Other people are also free agents, yet everything they do is ultimately controlled by God. If someone insults you or in some way harms you, know that this has been sent by God as a way to cleanse your soul. If things go against you, be patient. When you accept everything as God's will, this causes the veil of concealment to be removed, thus manifesting God's control over all creation (from "Seven Pillars of Faith" by Rabbi Yitzchak Breiter).

Although aggrieved, Joseph forgave his brothers completely and showed them the utmost love. He wanted them to repent for their own good. When they came under his power, he did not reprove them - for this is embarrassing to the wrongdoer. Instead, with consummate skill he manipulated them into a situation where they would see for themselves that they had committed a great wrong. Thus last week's portion (*Mikeitz*, Genesis 41:1-44:17) told how when Joseph first imprisoned his ten older brothers and kept one of them hostage to ensure that the others would bring Benjamin too down to Egypt, the brothers - who had also undoubtedly been reared on the above principles of faith - immediately realized that if they suffered such a reverse, it must be the hand of God.

"And each one said to his brothers, 'But it is we who are to blame because of our brother, the pain of whose soul we saw when he begged us and we did not listen. That is why this trouble has come upon us'" (Genesis 42:21).

The ensuing story traces the successive stages of Joseph's brothers' remorse, contrition and repentance, until in the end they admitted to him how terribly they had wronged him and literally begged him to forgive them and not to take revenge, as described in the concluding verses of the book of Genesis at the end of next week's portion (Genesis, 50:15-22). Penitent wrongdoers also display greatness - when they have the courage to admit their guilt and change their ways. This is an important lesson for all of us, because very few can honestly say that they are innocent of all wrong in their behavior towards others.

It is also an important lesson for leaders - for the qualities of true leadership are a central theme in the story of Joseph and his brothers. We live in an age where many of those charged with the leadership of countries and world blocs display a marked inability to admit their human fallibility or take responsibility for the huge errors and mistaken assumptions that have led us to the brink of world war, economic ruin and ecological disaster. Not only under dictatorial regimes but even in the supposedly "free" world, the mainstream media, which are largely controlled by the same interests that buttress the leadership, likewise cosmetically paper over their follies with "spin".

But the true leader is the first to admit his own wrong and sin before God, as in the immortal words of King David, exemplar of the Messianic King:

"Be gracious to me, O God, according to Your mercy; according to the multitude of Your compassions, blot out my transgressions. Wash me thoroughly from my iniquity and cleanse me from my sin. For I know my transgressions; and my sin is ever before me...Behold, You desire truth in the inward parts; make me, therefore, to know wisdom in my inmost heart. Create me a pure heart, O God; and renew a steadfast spirit within me...Then I will teach transgressors Your ways; and sinners shall return to You. O Lord, open my lips, and my mouth shall declare Your praise" (Psalms 51 vv 1-3, 6, 10, 13, 15).

Good Words

"Death and life are in the power of the tongue" (Proverbs 18:21).

The closing portion of the book of Genesis completes the story of the founding fathers of the Torah pathway, the patriarchs Abraham, Isaac and Jacob, with the account of Jacob's final blessings to his twelve sons prior to his death and burial in the Cave of Machpelah in Hebron.

Normally before the head of a family departs this life, he writes a "will", which may include wise advice and instructions for his offspring but most often is concerned primarily with the division of his estate. However, in our portion, with the exception of Jacob's special gift to Joseph of Shechem (Genesis 49:22) we do not hear of any disposition of material property among his sons. Rather, the climax of our portion comes with Jacob's sublimely poetical prophetic blessings to each of them in turn through which he established their future destinies in God's great scheme of history. If he castigated his first three sons over their misdeeds, he did not damn their souls forever; he cursed not them but only their misdirected anger. If he penalized them, it was by scattering them among the other tribes so that their very strength and power would radiate to all (Genesis 49:7).

The blessing and the curse

The history of humanity began with God's blessing to Adam and Eve and their descendants: "And God blessed them; and God said unto them: 'Be fruitful, and multiply, and replenish the earth, and subdue it; and have dominion over the fish of the sea, and over the fowl of the air, and over every living thing that creeps upon the earth'" (Genesis 1:28).

However, a crafty force of evil symbolized by the serpent "bit" into the souls of the once-innocent man and his wife, bringing the very opposite of blessing into the world: "And God said to the serpent: 'Because you have done this, you are cursed.' To the woman He said: 'I will greatly multiply your pain and travail.' And to the man He said: 'Cursed is the ground for your sake.' (ibid. 3:1-19).

On account of this curse, our lives in this world until this day are accompanied with much pain and travail as we toil to scrape a living and raise new generations. While a blessing is a formula of words that programmatically establishes a glorious future for the blessed, a curse is a poisonous formula aimed by the jealous enemy of the blessed to try to spoil that future.

The story of the Patriarchs traces how each in turn received the power of blessing. In God's opening challenge to Abraham to go to the Land, He said: "...you shall be a blessing; and I shall bless those that bless you, but those that curse you shall I curse, and through you shall all the families of the earth be blessed" (Genesis 12:2-3). From Abraham, the power of blessing passed to Isaac - "And after the death of Abraham, God blessed Isaac his son" (ibid. 25:11). Then Isaac gave the blessing to Jacob: "...and indeed he shall be blessed" (ibid. 27:33).

Abraham's nephew Laban, an idolatrous high priest and master of the occult arts, sought to wrest the power of blessing from Jacob and dispense his own blessings (Genesis 24:31). But Laban looked upon all of the world with an evil eye, the eye of envy and hatred, and was ready to curse his very daughters and all their children and descendants for ever on account of his jealousy of Jacob (Deuteronomy 26:5 and Rashi thereon). Even Laban's blessing to his own sister Rebecca (Genesis 24:60) turned into a curse, because she became barren until God Himself unraveled the curse (ibid. 25:21). Laban's heir in sorcery, Bilaam, sought to curse the Children of Israel, but God intervened and turned all his intended curses into blessings (Numbers 22:2-24:25).

The power of words

God created the world through speech, and the defining trait of His choicest creation, the human, is the gift of language with which He has endowed us. The account of Jacob's blessings in our present portion teaches the importance of carefully measuring our words and using their great power for good and not for evil.

The contemporary world is largely dominated by the sophisticated communications media which continually expose us to streams of words and other messages designed to capture our conscious or unconscious attention, lure and entice us and sweep us into the spin of the seller, promoter, politician or advertiser who wants to bring us under his sway. This constant abuse of language for gain makes many cynical.

The Torah teaches a higher use of human language: for prayer and communication with God; to give thanks and praise to God for the wonders of creation; to voice our hearts' hopes, longings and yearnings in requests, entreaties and supplications for what we need. Likewise, the words we speak to others in the course of our everyday lives in the home, the workplace, community and wider world should be intended to spread blessings and not the opposite.

When someone simply asks you how you are, Rabbi Nachman teaches us to answer carefully. "When someone asks his friend how he is and the friend says, 'Not good', this can be an opening for trouble because God says, 'You call this not good? I'll show you what not good is!'

But if when his friend asks how he is, he answers brightly, 'Good, thank God!' even though things really are not so good, God says, 'This you call good? I'll show you what good is!'" (Siach Sarfey Kodesh 1-32).

Many people think that in order to show humility, one must disparage oneself. This is not so. We must believe in ourselves and in the God-given goodness that lies in or very core. And since all those around us are God's creations, they must also contain good. We are not required to turn a blind eye to other's failings and weaknesses or pretend they are other than what they are. At the same time, we must have faith that they have good in them, and we should seek it out.

Too often the language with which people talk to and about one another is poisoned with explicit or implied accusation and verbal barbs intended to hurt. But in the language of blessing, words are used for their ameliorative effect - as when one person salutes another with Peace.

Thus did the ancient sages institute that a person should enquire after his friend's welfare invoking the name of God, as it is written: "And behold Boaz was coming from Bethlehem, and he said to the harvesters, 'God be with you', and they said to him, 'May God bless you'" (Ruth 2:4; Mishnah Berachot 9).

The tongue rules over all

Once the king of Persia was sick and the doctors told him: 'Your only cure is if they bring you milk of a lioness and then you will be healed.' Someone got up and said: 'I will bring you a lioness's milk if you want: give me ten goats.' The king instructed his servants to give them to him, and they did so. The man went to the lions' den. In the den was a lioness that was suckling her whelps. One day he stood at a distance and threw her one goat and she ate it. The next day he drew a little closer and threw her another. He did so until he was playing with her, and then he took some of her milk and went back.

Half way along the road, he had a dream in which his limbs were quarrelling. The legs were saying, 'None among all the limbs can be compared to us - if we had not gone there he would not have been able to get the milk.' The hands were saying, 'None is like us - if we had not done what we did nothing would have come of it.' The heart said: 'If I had not given you the plan, of what use would any of you have been?' Then the tongue spoke up and said: 'If I had not said the word, what would he have done?' All the other limbs answered: 'How dare you compare yourself to us when you dwell in a place of darkness and you have no counsel like the other limbs.' She said to them: 'Today you will admit that I am in control of you.'

The man heard these words and went to the king and said: "My lord the king, here is the milk of a *kalba* (dog)." The king was furious and ordered him to be hanged. As he went to his execution the limbs began to cry. The tongue said to them: 'Did I not tell you that you are useless. If I save you, you will know that I am above you.' 'Yes,' they said.

The man said to his executioners: 'Take me back to the king, maybe I will be saved.'

They brought him back, and he said to the king: 'Why did you give the order to hang me?' He said: 'Because you brought me the milk of a dog.' The man replied: 'What should that matter to you? This will heal you - people do call a lioness a *kalba* '. They took some of it and tested it and found it to be lioness's milk. The limbs said to the tongue: 'We hereby acknowledge that life and death are in the power of the tongue.

See! The tongue is greater than the sacrifices, for it says: "I shall praise the name of God in song and I shall magnify Him in thanks, and this will find greater favor from God than an ox offering" (Psalms 69:31-32; Midrash Yalkut Shimoni on Psalms #721).

The Call to Freedom

Much of the history of humanity has been the story of one person, group or nation ruling over others in various guises under different names. Very early on those who were more assertive took control over the more compliant, building great empires with complex hierarchies of leaders and subjects "from the firstborn of Pharaoh who sits on his throne to the firstborn of the slave woman that is behind the mill." (Exodus 11:5).

The first recorded Biblical tyrant was Nimrod, who was "a mighty hunter before God" ruling over a vast empire (Genesis 10:8-10). It is ironic that Nimrod was the son of Kush, firstborn son of Ham, whom Noah had cursed to be a slave of his more civilized brothers (ibid. 9:25-27). Likewise, Ham's second son Mitzraim - Egypt - spawned the greatest slave system of antiquity and held sway over the entire then-known world (Gen. 41:57).

As we now enter the book of Exodus, we embark on the story of God's overthrow of the Egyptian tyrant to redeem His "firstborn son" Israel (Ex. 4:22) from slavery. This drama takes up our present portion and the three that follow it, and is the central historical event and reference point throughout the rest of the Five Books of Moses, a paradigmatic tale of freedom that comes to teach all the generations until today.

The Exodus came to correct the very deep flaw in humanity through which "slaves go on horses while princes walk like slaves on the ground" (Ecclesiastes 10:7) - as when tyrannical rulers take control and tread precious souls underfoot the sake of their own mundane power, pleasure, wealth and glory. The story of the Exodus offers eternal hope to all humanity that the different kinds of oppressive tyrannies that keep people enslaved physically and mentally will eventually be cast down, just as "the horse and its rider did He cast into the sea" (Exodus 15:1) revealing the truth that no mortal can truly rule, because only "God will rule forever and ever" (ibid. v. 18).

The Torah certainly favors enlightened government, as in the reign of King Solomon, who "held sway over the whole of the west of the Euphrates. and was at peace with all his subjects around" (I Kings 5:4). But the exile of Israel under Pharoah in Egypt was the paradigm of tyranny gone mad, where the government begins to oppress and even exterminate its own population for fear of a revolution (Exodus 1:22).

The Children of Israel were the seed of the illustrious Patriarchs, yet in Exile in Egypt they fell to a level where they themselves felt compelled to serve their masters. Similarly throughout history until today many of the oppressed tend to internalize their oppressors' perceptions of them. It is not only through conquest that one group or people are forced to submit to another. Often the ruled endure their degradation for the sake of supposed protection, livelihood and other benefits for which they hope for from their rulers.

Moses came not to instigate a political slave rebellion but to shift a whole generation's perception of what is the purpose of our lives in this world. The Children of Israel walked out free from Egypt when they witnessed God submitting the lives and ecology of their Egyptian masters to massive attacks from every direction, proving that it is not man who rules but God alone, and Israel preferred to serve this God.

Freedom is a term that has many different connotations for different people. The freedom to which God called Israel was not the freedom to do as you please and follow every human impulse no matter where it may lead. Nor was it only the simple political freedom to which many aspire, for God's freedom can be experienced even under oppression and in slavery. This is because God's freedom is an internal attitude of freedom from the mundane world that is granted within us to the extent that we are willing to submit ourselves to God's rule and His Code.

When God called Moses to his mission to save the Children of Israel, He guaranteed him that the proof of the divinity of his ministry would come when he would "bring the people out of Egypt and they will serve God on this mountain" (Exodus

3:12) - Mount Sinai, where Israel would later receive the Torah. The purpose of the Exodus was not to grant license to do anything one wishes, but to bring the people to a higher service, the service of the One God, that would free them from mental servitude to the mundane world.

The Torah for Israel and the Seven Universal Laws for the Children of Noah, the nations of the world, are the Code of service to the One God that grants freedom from mundane service. Even under actual servitude, the servant of God is not a servant of man.

Thus the rabbis tell that when the tyrant king of Babylon, Nebuchadnezzar, threatened to burn Daniel's three companions alive if they would not bow to his idol (Daniel ch. 3), they replied: "You may be king over us when it comes to taxes, but to govern us in services and beliefs, you and a dog are equal" (Vayikra Rabba #33, Bamidbar #15).

True inner freedom comes through submission to the service of God by following His commandments.

A Stark Warning

The dramatic story of the redemption of the enslaved people of Israel from their Egyptian masters takes up the first four portions of the book of Exodus. Of these, the second - our present portion - and the one that follows it describe in graphic detail the series of Ten Plagues with which God struck Egypt until they capitulated and sent their slaves forth to freedom. Our present portion tells of the first seven plagues, while the one that follows describes the last three.

The drama of the plagues is central to the entire Torah: What does it come to teach us?

The narrative is not addressed to Israel alone, even though they were the ones who were redeemed. They played a relatively passive role in their redemption. They cried out to God over their plight (Exodus 2:23), and when Moses and Aaron came to their elders announcing their imminent redemption, they had faith and believed (ibid. 4:30-31). Yet in the entire drama of the Ten Plagues, the Israelites did little but witness events. It was Moses who stood forth to warn Pharaoh to repent, raising his rod to invoke each plague. Only prior to the last plague, the death of the Egyptian firstborn, did the Israelites slaughter their paschal lambs, and the next morning they marched out of

Egypt to freedom carrying their un-risen, hastily baked bread on their backs (Exodus ch 12).

The supreme might that God displayed in each of the successive plagues was certainly intended to leave its mark on the Israelites and their descendants for ever: "That you may tell in the ears of your son and your son's son what I have done in Egypt and My signs which I have worked among them, that you may know that I am the Lord" (Ex. 10:2). "And you shall tell your son on that day, saying 'It is because of what the Lord did for me when I came out of Egypt' (Ex. 13:8).

But the Plagues were also sent to teach a great lesson to Pharaoh himself, to the Egyptians, and to all humanity for ever after.

God could have brought one cataclysmic disaster upon Egypt and released the Israelite slaves in a moment. Instead He sent a succession of successively more invasive plagues, giving Pharaoh a respite and an opportunity to repent each time. God told Pharaoh that the reason He let him survive was precisely to show him His might: "But in very deed for this cause have I made you stand, to show you My power, and that My name may be declared throughout all the earth" (Ex. 9:16). The lesson of the Ten Plagues is for everyone.

The archetypal rebel

In the previous portion we read that when Moses came to Pharaoh the first time to ask him in the name of HaShem to release Israel from their bondage, Pharaoh answered: "Who is HaShem that I should listen to His voice to let Israel go? I do not know HaShem, and moreover I will not let Israel go!" (Ex. 5:2).

With these words Pharaoh showed himself the archetype of the self-willed human who arrogantly rebels against his Maker regardless of the fact that God always has the upper hand since He controls all creation, and will sooner or later kill this creature - because no human can escape death. "See now that I, even I, am He, and there is no god with Me; I kill, and I make alive; I have wounded, and I heal; and there is none that can deliver out of My hand (Deuteronomy 32:39).

God in His goodness initially uses kind and gentle ways to bring us to know and serve Him. But if we are stubborn and will not acknowledge Him, if we refuse to bend our will to His, He may show us greater and greater force, as in the narrative of the plagues, where God attacks Pharaoh from every direction through His many agents and emissaries, the armies of humble frogs, the swarms of gnats and locusts, the wild animals, the catastrophic hail, the minute "viruses" that caused the infectious cattle and sheep disease and the boils...

Under the full fire of each plague in its time Pharaoh would momentarily relent: "And Pharaoh sent and called for Moses and Aaron, and said to them: 'I have sinned this time; HaShem is righteous, and I and my people are wicked."

(Ex. 9:27). But as soon as the crisis passed, Pharaoh's heart was again hardened, and he reverted to his view that the plagues were mere "chance", "bad luck" containing no lesson or message, as if the world has no Judge.

But the Torah warns: "And if you walk *contrary* to Me and will not listen to Me, I will bring seven times more plagues upon you according to your sins. And if in spite of these things you will not be corrected to Me but will walk *contrary* to Me, then will I also walk *contrary* unto you, and I will strike you, even I, seven times for your sins. (Leviticus ch 26 vv 21-24).

In the biblical Hebrew, the word translated in the above text as "contrary" is **keri**, which has the connotation of "chance". If people believe that all is "chance" and "luck" with no law and no Judge - a belief that permits one to use any means to attain one's objectives - God may use all manner of "chance occurrences" and "accidents" to chastise them. In order to test us, this world is evidently arranged so that many things appear to happen "by chance". Yet beneath the veil of material "reality" stands the all-powerful controlling "hand" of God Almighty.

Even the greatest and most powerful people must understand that they are but instruments in the hands of God to work His purpose. How much more so must ordinary people recognize that we are His creations and are duty bound to serve Him. The story of the catastrophe that Pharaoh brought upon himself and all Egypt through his stubborn rebellion against God comes to teach us all a stark lesson in the fear of God Almighty.

"Should the axe boast itself against the one that hews with it? Should the saw magnify itself against the one that moves it? As if a rod should move those that lift it up, or as if a staff should lift up the one that is not wood" (Isaiah 10:15).

"But the wicked are like the troubled sea; for it cannot rest, and its waters cast up mire and dirt" (Isaiah 57:20).

"Just like the sea, where the waves rise up proudly each in turn, but as each wave reaches the sand it is broken and retreats, but the wave that follows it sees how it was broken yet he too arrogantly rises up and refuses to back down - so are the wicked. They see each other's destruction yet they still rise up arrogantly, and that is why they are compared to the sea" (Midrash Tanchuma, Leviticus 7).

Boundaries

We see in the account of the Ten Plagues and the Exodus that God repeatedly discriminated between the Egyptian masters - who were stricken - and their Israelite slaves, who were saved. This happened in the case of the plague of wild animals (Ex. 8:18-19), the pestilence that afflicted the Egyptian livestock (ibid 9:4, 6), the hail (ibid. v. 26), the darkness (10:23), and most strikingly, the death of the Egyptian firstborn as related in our portion.

Another kind of discrimination between Israel and all the other nations appears in the institution of the sacrificial Passover lamb that the Israelites were commanded to eat annually in Temple times to commemorate the Exodus:

"And God said to Moses and Aaron, This is the statute of the Paschal Lamb: No alien may eat from it. No uncircumcised male may eat from it" (Exodus 12:43, 48). Only Israelite females and males that had been duly circumcised were allowed to partake of the meat of the sacrifice.

Thus the Torah Code as it applies to Israel, which begins to unfold in our present portion and is elaborated in all the remainder of the Five Books of Moses, may appear to be highly exclusive and even racist in its discrimination between members of the people of Israel and other peoples.

That a religious pathway should be open only to members of one people while apparently excluding all others runs contrary to the modern egalitarian doctrine that "all men are created equal". For this reason many throughout the world reject the Torah, feeling it has no place for them. Others have claimed that because the people of Israel sinned, God's covenant with them was rescinded and that the Community of Israel is now open to all gentiles and the Torah belongs to all.

The 613 Commandments that God gave to Israel are indeed a highly rigorous code with many demands and many restrictions. If the Israelites had hitherto been slaves of the Egyptians, their Exodus was no release to a life of freedom in the sense of license to do as you please. Having been saved by God, they and their descendants were beholden to Him and obliged to serve Him.

Adherence to this code with all its demands is not required of other peoples, but they are by no means excluded from accepting it and becoming fully-fledged Israelites, as long as they are willing to embrace the 613 commandments in their entirety.

Thus our portion states explicitly: "And when a stranger shall dwell with you and will keep the Passover to HaShem, let all his males be circumcised, and then let him come near and keep it; and he shall be as one that is born in the land. There shall be one law for a person that is home-born and for the stranger that dwells among you" (Exodus 12:48-9).

One and the same Torah applies equally to a person who is Israelite by birth and to a righteous convert (*Ger Tzeddek*) - one who has accepted the Torah code in full. This is surely perfectly egalitarian and does not fly in the face of the modern outlook any more than the idea that the doctors are entitled to put the most stringent demands on anyone who wants to practice medicine while no-one is excluded if they submit to those demands.

The exclusion of anyone who is not a circumcised Israelite or a full convert from certain Torah commandments including the Passover lamb is thus quite different from racism of the kind practiced by the Nazis, where no non-Aryan could ever "convert" or be accepted as a member of the "master race".

Membership of the people of Israel by birth is not in itself any guarantee of God's salvation or a place in the life of the world to come. Home-born Israelites and converts are equally subject to the stringencies of the Torah code, where infringement of God's commandments may be punished by penalties in this world and after death.

When a gentile comes seeking conversion to Judaism, he is warned: "Know that before you enter this religion, if you eat the *cheilev* - fat of an animal you will not be punished with spiritual excision after death, and if you desecrate the Sabbath you are not liable to the penalty of death by stoning, but now after you convert, if you eat that fat you will be punished with excision and if you desecrate the Sabbath you are liable to the penalty of stoning" (Maimonides, Mishneh Torah, Laws of Forbidden Unions 14:2).

The worst of all penalties for an Israelite is to have no share in the eternal life of the World to Come. Among the transgressions that would cause an Israelite to lose his share in the World to Come are: atheism; idolatry; denial of the divinity of one or more of the commandments or even of one verse or one word of the Torah, denial of prophecy, of the received Oral Torah, of the coming resurrection of the dead and of Messiah (Maimonides, Mishneh Torah, Laws of Repentance chapter 3).

The 613 Commandments are not a kind a religious smorgasbord from which one may pick and choose what to observe according to one's fancy. Those who believe they are Israelites without submitting to all the stringencies of the Torah code as explained by its sages are simply deceiving themselves.

God has not demanded that other peoples submit themselves to Him as His "servants" in precisely the same way that he makes this demand of Israel. Yet those from other peoples are free to become His servants if they so wish in one of two ways. Some may choose to convert to Judaism, but the Torah by no means requires this, for it provides the gentiles with their own many-faced pathway through the Seven Universal Laws of the Children of Noah with all their ramifications.

And "Everyone who embraces the Seven Commandments and is careful to practice them is one of the saints of the nations of the world and has a share in the World to Come" (Maimonides, Laws of Kings 8:11).

"Sing praises to God, sing praises; sing praises to our King, sing praises. For God is the King of all the earth; sing praises in a skillful song. God reigns over the nations; G-d sits upon His holy throne. The noble princes of the peoples are gathered together, the people of the God of Abraham; for to God belong the shields of the earth; He is greatly exalted" (Psalm 47:7-10).

Faith and Trust

The three main narratives in our portion - about the crossing of the Red Sea, the Manna that sustained Israel in the wilderness and the war of Amalek - come to teach fundamental lessons about Faith and Trust that relate to all people.

The Splitting of the Sea

The simultaneous redemption of Israel and destruction of their Egyptian oppressors through the splitting of the Red Sea was a miracle that sent reverberations through the entire world: "The peoples heard, they tremble; pangs have taken hold of the inhabitants of Philistia" (Exodus 15:14).

For people today who have been schooled in the scientific study of the laws of nature, the destructive Tsunamis of recent years have made it easier to accept that a freak event like the splitting of the Red Sea is far from being impossible. The real miracle was not so much that the waters parted, but that they did so precisely when the people of Israel were in direst need as they stood trapped between the pursuing Egyptians and the deep blue sea. At that moment Israel saw clearly that He who created the laws of nature has the power to bend them at will.

"And Israel saw the great might which God used against the Egyptians, and the people feared God; and they *believed* in God and in His servant Moses" (ibid. 14:31).

The miracle came to inculcate the newly-freed nation with *faith* in God and in His omnipotent power. It showed that nature is not blind and indifferent to humans and their struggles; rather it is a veil through which God exercises His supreme power - often in very inscrutable ways - for the benefit of His creations, in order to bring them under the wing of His higher law, the Torah.

The splitting of the Red Sea was an outstanding one-time miracle that came to demonstrate for all the generations that God has absolute omnipotence. It was necessary to show that God is in complete control of everything, including the seemingly implacable laws of nature, in order to open people's eyes to the fact that even when things go "normally", God's miracles and His benevolent providence are present at all times.

Having a general belief in God's existence is the foundation of a life of faith in harmony with His law, but it is only the beginning. After coming to believe in God in a general way, it is necessary to learn that God is not merely a great power somewhere out there in heaven, but that He is in complete control of every single detail of creation down here on earth at all times.

When we understand this we know that we are not alone and abandoned, but that our Father in Heaven is involved with us and cares about us at every step in our lives. This should encourage us to follow God's laws as they apply in all the different junctures of our lives, thereby drawing His blessing into all that we do. General faith thus turns into trust in God in all the specifics of our lives. The more we do what we do under the guidance of His laws and teachings, the more we become connected to Him through the very details of this world, and our knowledge of Him becomes ever deepened.

The Manna

Thus the great lesson of faith in God taught through the splitting of the Red Sea was followed by a long, protracted lesson in trusting Him day after day for one's very livelihood as the Children of Israel now began to journey deeper into the wilderness on their way to the Promised Land.

Within three days in the arid wilderness they were faced with their first test when they had no water with which to quench their thirst. They now had to learn that He who split the waters of the Red Sea also has the power to provide water in the desert and even to turn bitter waters into sweet, as he did at Marah:

"There He made for them a statute and an ordinance, and there He tested them; and He said: If you will diligently hearken to the voice of

HaShem your God and will do what is right in His eyes, and attend to His commandments, and observe all His statutes, I will not put upon you all the diseases which I have put upon the Egyptians; for I am HaShem that heals you" (ibid. 15:25-6).

According to received Torah tradition, the "statute" and the "ordinance" that God laid down for Israel at Marah included *Dinim* - the basic laws governing people's relations with each other, such as the prohibition of theft and robbery, compensation for damages etc., which are subsumed under the general Noahide law prohibiting stealing.

Immediately after the people received these first laws, they were faced with their next great test - having nothing to eat in the wilderness. The miraculous way in which God fed Israel with the mysterious Manna that condensed on the ground around the camp every morning came to teach that even in the most desperate conditions, God still has the power to sustain us. There is therefore no need to take what we require by force - through theft and robbery - because God can provide us with everything we really need benignly and easily. For God provides for all his creatures "from the horns of the wild ox to the eggs of lice".

One who steals demonstrates a lack of belief in God's omnipotence and His ability to provide us with what we need through legitimate means. For this reason the Torah sages taught that a trader who short-sells the public through the use of deceptive weights and measures is in denial of the

Exodus from Egypt (Maimonides, Laws of Theft 7:12) - because he does not believe that God's omnipotent power includes the ability to give him profit without forcing the issue through deception. The trader thinks that the public will not notice - but God sees.

The war of Amalek

If God were visible to us at all times there would be no merit in having faith and trust in Him. The manifest salvation of the splitting of the Red Sea could not be repeated every day. Indeed God often *hides* Himself in order to increase our merit in having to believe in Him even when we do not see Him. Thus Israel reached the point where they came to doubt whether God was with them or not (Exodus 17:7). This was what led to the attack by Amalek, the archetype of denial and atheism.

"And it was when Moses raised his hand that Israel prevailed, but when he relaxed his hand Amalek prevailed.

"How could it be that Moses hands won the war or lost the war? Rather, this comes to tell you that as long as Israel directed their eyes above and submitted their hearts to their Father in Heaven they prevailed, but if not, they fell" (Rosh Hashanah 3:8).

The struggle against the atheist and denier that resides in our hearts continues every day. We win the battle when we raise our inner eye of faith to

God at every juncture and fortify ourselves in the knowledge that God is with us at all times.

Courts of Law

It is testimony to the universality of the Torah that the very portion which describes the election of Israel as God's "kingdom of priests" through the Covenant at Sinai is named after the world's greatest high-priest of idolatry, Yitro - Jethro - who on hearing of God's miracles for Israel and the justice He brought upon Egypt, became a convert to the Torah of HaShem.

And lest the convert imagine that as one who has entered Israel from the outside, he could never be fully accepted into the fold, our portion shows that "Yitro added a section to the Torah" (Midrash Mekhilta) - for it was upon his suggestion that the Israelite system of leadership and justice was instituted. Moses' prophecy would always be the ultimate source of authority, but the burden of leadership would be shared and delegated to successive ranks of leaders, judges and magistrates (Exodus 18:13-26).

An important interpretational rule used by the Torah sages is that "there is no before and after in the Torah". What this means is that although the Biblical stories appear to be arranged in a chronological sequence, there are sections where something that actually occurred at a later point in time is told at an earlier point in the text on account of its thematic relationship with the adjacent passages. A case in point is this very section dealing with the judiciary, which immediately follows the account of Jethro's arrival in the wilderness to search for the truth, as narrated in Exodus 18:1-12.

"And it was on *the day afterwards* that Moses sat to judge the people, and the people stood around Moses from the morning to the evening..." (Exodus 18:13).

From a casual glance at the text it might seem as if "the day afterwards" was the day after Jethro's arrival in the wilderness, as described in the previous verses. However, the Torah sages demonstrated that Jethro's advice about appointing judges could only have been offered at some date *after* the Giving of the Torah, even though the latter is described at a later point in the text in chapters 19-20. The reason is that in the section on the judiciary (chapter 18 verse 16), Moses refers to "God's statutes and teachings" which he had to teach the people, and these were given only at Sinai (see Rashi on Exodus 18:1).

Jethro watched the throngs of people pressing in on Moses to ask how the Torah code applied in practice to each one's personal issues. With the fresh, clear vision of an "outsider", Jethro immediately grasped that the crushing burden of communal responsibility would quickly wear out Moses unless - with God's consent - he would choose fitting leaders to whom to delegate his authority.

"You must caution them about the statutes and the teachings and make known to them the path they must follow and the actions they must take. And you look out from all the people for men of valor who fear God, men of truth who hate corrupt gain, and appoint them as captains of thousands, captains of hundreds, captains of fifties and captains of tens. And they shall judge the people at all times and all major matters they shall bring to you and every small thing they shall adjudicate..." (Ex. 18, 20-22).

Despite the fact that, as explained above, chronologically Jethro's proposal could only have been made *after* the Giving of the Torah, its thematic importance is so great that in the Torah text it is positioned *before* and as an an *introduction* to the account of the Giving of the Torah. This is because a duly constituted judiciary composed of men of integrity is the very found-ation for the establishment of a viable universal Torah code that will bring genuine peace among all people.

There is a natural tendency for people to be refractory, and a system of law can only rein in their baser aspects with efficient policing and a fair, swift, scrupulous judiciary.

The institution of courts of law and justice is the seventh of the Noahide Commandments. It was given to Jethro - a Noahide and a former explorer of all the different human pathways to the divine - to introduce the concept of a hierarchical system of judges of integrity into the Torah code. Perhaps this great merit was given to Jethro because in all he heard about God's overthrow of Egypt - the greatest superpower of his era - he recognized that the true greatness of HaShem above all other powers was revealed through His justice: "Now I know that HaShem is great above all the gods for [He dealt with the Egyptians] through the very thing with which they schemed against them" [i.e. against the Israelites, namely through water, in which the Egyptians sought to drown the Israelite babies. So did He deal with the Egyptians, measure for measure, drowning them in the sea]" (Ex. 18:11 as explained by the Targum).

In verse 21, Jethro succinctly summarizes the three essential qualities that people must have in order to qualify to serve as judges over others. Firstly, they must be "God-fearing" - that is to say, they must fear to do any wrong even when no human can see them, because they know that God's all-seeing eye takes in everything and He eventually brings everyone to justice. Secondly, they must be "men of truth" - they must earnestly seek out the real truth of each matter and not content themselves with superficial appearances and circumstantial evidence. Thirdly, they must be people that "hate corrupt gain".

This has the greatest relevance in our times, when some of the most "advanced" blocs and countries in the world (such as the European Union and Great Britain) have been rocked with scandals involving the embezzlement of enormous sums from tax-payers' pockets through false expenses claims by their very legislators and members of parliament. There is also much evidence that prominent members of the governments, judiciaries and police forces of such countries permit extraneous interests to influence their decisions, with preferential treatment being accorded to some and commissions of enquiry that cover up much more than they expose.

Where corrupt vested interests are deeply entrenched, it takes great courage to protest. The Torah itself is an eternal protest against the corruption of leaders and judges.

The Sinaitic Covenant

The narrative of the event known as the Giving of the Torah - when all the people of Israel stood at Mount Sinai, heard the voice of HaShem and undertook to observe all His commandments - is spread over two Torah portions: the previous portion of *Yitro* and our present portion of *Mishpatim*.

In *Yitro*, Exodus chapter 19 told of the assembly of the Children of Israel at the foot of Sinai and of Moses' ascent to the summit of the mountain, while chapter 20 set forth the 10 Commandments, describing the awesome and literally earth-shaking experience when they were revealed.

Then in our present portion of *Mishpatim*, chapters 21-23 - which make up the greater part of the portion - set forth a multitude of very detailed laws for the Children of Israel, after which the closing section of our portion, Exodus chapter 24, reverts to the narrative of the Giving of the Torah, telling how Moses struck a formal Covenant between God and the Children of Israel to observe this code of law.

The sandwiching of the detailed laws contained in Exodus chapters 21-23 in between the narrative of the Giving of the Torah contained in *Yitro* chapter 19 and the narrative in *Mishpatim* chapter 24, indicates that these detailed laws are no less integral to the Sinaitic Code than the Ten Commandments. Further exposition of all these laws and their ramifications is contained in the other legal sections of the Five Books of Moses, and especially in Leviticus 19-20 and Deuteronomy chapters 12-25.

While the 613 Commandments of the Torah are mandatory only for Israel, the Sinaitic Covenant is of great importance for all peoples and nations, because proper understanding of God's laws for all the nations - the Seven Universal Noahide Commandments - depends upon proper understanding of His laws for Israel. This is because the Seven Universal Laws are the roots of the entire Torah, and all of the 613 Commandments that apply to Israel stem from these roots. Thus the details of the 613 Commandments shed great light on how the general laws of the Noahide Code are to be applied in practice.

Among the detailed commandments in our present portion of *Mishpatim* there are many that have a direct bearing on the practical application of the Noahide laws prohibiting idolatry, blasphemy, murder, incest, robbery and cruelty to animals as well as the institution of courts of law.

Thus Exodus 21:12-14 differentiates between intentional murder and unintentional manslaughter, which relates to the Noahide prohibition of killing; verses 18-36 enter into the details of the laws of various kinds of damages to person and property, which relate to the Noahide provision for a system of justice. Exodus 21:37-22:14 deals with the detailed laws of theft, which are bound up with the Noahide prohibition of theft; Exodus chapter 23 verses 1-3 and 7-9 relate to legal procedure in courts of law, and so on.

The correct interpretation of the Divine Writ according to a system of exegetical rules has been a labor of love of Torah scholars for thousands of years, and many thick volumes of Talmudic discussion together with an enormous literature of commentaries and legal decisions are devoted to establishing the fine details of all of these laws and how they are to be applied in practical cases in all their variety in actual life.

One of the great challenges facing today's Torah scholars is to define in detail how the Seven Noahide Laws are to be applied today in practical contemporary cases in the light of the relevant laws in the Sinaitic code. This process has now begun as a number of Rabbis under the auspices of the renewed Sanhedrin in Jerusalem are addressing numerous questions being received from growing numbers of gentiles who seriously seek to observe the Noahide laws in the proper way.

Intricate legal issues can only be adjudicated by trained legal minds, and the general student cannot expect to be able to determine matters of

Torah law on his or her own without expert guidance.

Nevertheless the Five Books of Moses are available to all the world in translations into many different languages, and some of the classical rabbinical commentaries are also available in English, French, Spanish, Russian etc. This means that gentiles may also study these works and gain insights into the meaning and application of the Seven Noahide Laws from seeing how the Torah teaches about their extrapolation in the 613 Commandments that apply to Israel.

Historically, one of the criticisms directed by some against the Torah pathway was that it consists of too many detailed rules and restrictions that inhibit the instinctive love and passion with which we should serve God. Ironically, the modern world - which has to a large extent thrown off the yoke of religious law and observance - suffers from an endless proliferation of governmental and other regulations and restrictions in every sphere of life down to the most intimate.

The promise of the Sinaitic Code is to give inner freedom and liberation to those who take upon themselves the service of God. Likewise submission to the supreme power of God through embrace of the Noahide Code elevates the righteous of the nations above subordinate powers.

The desire to obey and fulfill God's law is nurtured through regular study of the scriptures and derivative works, each on his or her level. For the more we become familiar with its details and the deeper our understanding of its intent and great wisdom, the stronger our love becomes.

The House of Prayer

"For My house will be called the House of Prayer
for all the Nations" (Isaiah 56:7)

The central theme of all the remaining five portions of the book of Exodus is the design, construction and inauguration of the Wilderness Sanctuary. The first six portions of the book of Leviticus then set forth the various priestly sacrificial and other rituals that were to be carried out there.

The attention and detail which the Torah devotes to the Sanctuary is a sign of its supreme importance. The Wilderness Sanctuary and its services stand as the prototype of the two Temples that later stood in Jerusalem, as well as of the Future Temple that is destined to stand in Jerusalem at the end of days, as foretold by the prophets of Israel (e.g. Isaiah 2:2ff, Micah 4:1ff, Ezekiel chs 40-48; see Maimonides, Laws of the Temple 1:4).

"Once the Temple was built in Jerusalem it was forbidden to built a house to HaShem in all other places or offer sacrifices to HaShem in them; and for all the generations there can be no other house except in Jerusalem alone and on Mount Moriah, of which it is said: 'And David said, This is the House of HaShem The God and this is the Altar of the burnt offering for Israel' (I Chronicles 22:1), and it says: 'This is My resting place until eternity' (Psalms 132:14)" (Maimonides ibid. 1:3).

The Sanctuary described in our portion was constructed entirely through the contributions of the people of Israel, and likewise the Temples in Jerusalem were built by Israel. The Temple services were and will be entrusted to the hands of the descendants of Aaron the High Priest - a select breed known as the Cohanim (priests), assisted by members of the rest of the tribe of Levi acting as the Temple singers and guards.

Yet while Israel are charged with the building and maintenance of the Temple, it is a place of the utmost significance for all the nations. This is because the intent of all the Temple services is to bring divine blessing and sustenance to all the different branches of creation in all places on earth - on the inanimate, vegetable, animal and human levels. All these levels were represented in the Temple services through the salt (Leviticus 2:13, inanimate level), offerings of grain, wine, oil and first fruits (vegetable level), the animal and bird sacrifices (animal level) and the priests and Levites conducting the services (human level). During the Festival of Succot, a total of 70 oxen were offered in the Temple on behalf of the 70 nations of the world (Numbers 29:13-32). The Rabbis taught: "If the nations of the world had understood how valuable the Holy Temple was for them, they would have surrounded it with troops and fortifications to guard it" (*Midrash Rabbah Numbers* 1:3) .

Thus the study of the details of the Wilderness prototype sanctuary and its services in this and the coming portions is of relevance to people of all nations, because the Temple and its offerings are replete with lessons about how we should lead our lives.

Our present portion begins by describing some of the main Sanctuary utensils. At the head comes the Ark of the Covenant, which contained the Two Tablets of Stone and the complete scroll of the Five Books of Moses. This is followed by the Showbread Table (representing material sustenance) and the Menorah Candelabrum (representing spiritual blessing). Our portion goes on to describe the structure of the Wilderness Sanctuary or "Tent of Meeting", with its layers of embroidered cloths and skins supported on walls formed by massive vertical gold-plated timbers. In the innermost part of the Sanctuary - the Holy of Holies - stood the Ark of the Covenant veiled by a curtain. In front of this curtain in the main sanctuary stood the Showbread Table to the right, the Candelabrum to the left and the golden incense altar (described later on in Exodus 30:1-5) in the middle. Outside the entrance to the Sanctuary in the open air stood the main altar for animal, bird, grain, oil and wine offerings. Both the Sanctuary and the Altar were enclosed in a courtyard.

The position of the Ark of the Covenant in the holiest part of the Sanctuary teaches us the supreme reverence that we must give to the Torah contained within it, since God's law is the prescription for peace and blessing for all the world. The Torah is the first of the three pillars on which the world stands (Avot 1:2; see Torah For the Nations commentary on Bereishit, "Torah study and the dignity of man").

The Sanctuary itself was not a place for congregational prayer as such. Ordinary Israelites were forbidden to enter there, and even the priests could enter only for the purpose of performing their services, such as lighting the candelabrum, burning the incense and placing the showbread, or to prostrate briefly.

The focal point of the Temple services was the outside Altar, where the priests would offer the sacrifices while a choir of Levites chanted. Since the offering of sacrifices anywhere but in the Temple was strictly forbidden, as explained above, it cannot be that the purpose of studying the Temple services is to enable people to imitate them elsewhere. Rather, the Temple sacrifices stand as a vivid symbol of the way humans should strive constantly to metaphorically "slaughter" and restrain their own lower "animal" instincts in order to elevate their higher human strengths and powers to the service of God.

"For You do not delight in sacrifice, or else would I give it; You have no pleasure in burnt-offering. The sacrifices of G-d are a broken spirit; a broken and a contrite heart, O God, You will not despise" (Psalms 51:18-19).

The most acceptable human offering to God is the prayers that we offer with deep veneration, humility, yearning and longing, in honesty and truth, from the innermost recesses of our hearts.

The Priesthood

Our portion is mostly devoted to the call of Aaron and his sons to the priesthood, the garments they were to wear when serving in the Sanctuary, and the instructions for their inauguration into this unique service.

Just as God chose Moses to receive and teach the Torah, so He chose Aaron - Moses' brother, his senior, and a prophet in his own right - to serve in His chosen sanctuary, and to be the progenitor of all later Israelite priests.

Contrary to contemporary notions of egalitarianism, membership of the Israelite priesthood was hereditary. The greatest merit, righteousness, Torah wisdom and purity could not make a Jew eligible to be a priest - a "Cohen", (plural: Cohanim) - unless his father and father's fathers had been valid Cohanim with impeccable patrilineal descent tracing back to Aaron, the first High Priest. (The Cohanim are permitted to marry women who are not daughters of Cohanim, and as long as the Cohen's wife is not defined as an improper woman or otherwise disqualified in Torah terms, his sons from her would be eligible to serve in the Temple.)

The Cohanim have two main functions:

1. They are charged with offering the blood and meat of the animal sacrifices and conducting all the other Temple services except for the singing and most of the ceremonial guard duties (which are in the hands of members of the tribe of Levy - the Levites). The Temple services are very onerous, requiring intense mental concentration as well as a variety of practical skills. The priests bear responsibility for bringing atonement for penitent sinners and for the entire community.

2. The Cohanim have the responsibility of teaching Torah to the people.

To enable the Cohanim to discharge these duties without having the burden of earning their living as well, the Torah laid down a variety of gifts that the rest of the people are obliged to give them for their basic maintenance and that of their families. These included certain sacrificial portions and other portions of meat and tithes ("Terumah") from crops for their food, and fleece of sheep for their clothing.

The Cohanim are not permitted to serve in the Temple or even eat their tithes - their very food - except when in a state of ritual purity in accordance with Torah law, which required constant ablutions in water as well as keeping their distance from things that ordinary people do not even think about. For example, it would be enough for a Cohen to have momentary physical contact with someone else that had been in the same building as a dead body (e.g. in a hospital), or to sit on his wife's chair or bed or touch her garment during her menstrual period, to make him ritually impure until he underwent the necessary procedure of purification in each case.

In Temple times, the entire priesthood was divided into twenty-four priestly watches, each of which took charge of the Temple services for an entire week in rotation. This meant that most Cohanim served in the Temple for only two weeks in the year and on the main festivals. For the rest of the time they lived dispersed throughout the Land of Israel. Each of the priests was responsible for visiting the local farms in order to collect their tithes and other priestly gifts. This brought them in constant contact with the people, to whom it was their responsibility to teach the Torah.

What can the Gentile learn from the Israelite priesthood?

Many Jewish communities until today include members who have a tradition from their fathers that they are Cohanim and who are honored as such (e.g. by being called first to the public reading of the Torah, although the system of priestly tithes is mostly in suspension today as we do not have the means of purification from defilement from the dead). Some maintain that certain genes are shared by all Cohanim, but only when Messiah comes and builds the coming

Temple in Jerusalem will the true descendants of Aaron be known for certain.

Sacrifices

These true descendants of Aaron alone will be entrusted with the conduct of the Temple services, and all others, whether Israelites or Gentiles, will be excluded from this by decree of the Torah. It is noteworthy that in strict practical terms, the Gentile today may have more to learn from the Cohen about sacrifices than the Jew who is not a Cohen. This is because Torah law forbids the Jew from offering any animal sacrifice either in Jerusalem or anywhere else, while it permits the Gentile to offer a burnt offering in any suitable place anywhere in the world (Maimonides, Laws of Sacrificial Procedure 19:16). With God's help, this will be discussed at greater length in our commentary on the first portion of Leviticus.

Teaching

Of greater practical relevance to the majority of people today is the role of the Cohen as teacher of Torah. This requires him to separate himself from the surrounding mundane world of self-indulgence, parties and entertainment in order to maintain the seriousness, devotion, purity and mental clarity that are necessary in order to study, understand and expound upon God's Law.

Unlike the Temple services, the study and teaching of Torah are certainly not restricted to Cohanim.

Every Israelite is obliged to study the 613 Commandments in all their ramifications to the best of his ability. Likewise every Gentile is obliged to know the Seven Universal Commandments, and every Gentile lover of HaShem surely wants to broaden and deepen his or her understanding of God's Torah for the nations to the greatest possible extent. For both Jews and Gentiles, only assiduous study can produce worthy teachers, who are vitally needed for the transmission and dissemination of the Torah.

In simpler times, outstanding Torah scholars and teachers earned their livings as workers, farmers, craftsmen and the like, and would have recoiled from the thought of receiving a stipend for their studies (although Torah judges are entitled to due compensation for the time they devote to legal cases). However, the sophistication and complexity of the modern world results in most people being required to undergo lengthy training for highly specialized and demanding work consuming the best of their waking hours. This makes it very difficult for the majority of adults to devote themselves to sustained Torah study to the level necessary to be capable of teaching others.

In the modern age of specialization, the Jewish people and the Gentile Nations are in need of full-time and part-time professional Torah teachers and disseminators of the Torah who are financially able to devote themselves to their calling through receiving the support of their communities, just as the Temple Cohanim received their maintenance from the surrounding farmers.

Thus, Rabbis of the necessary caliber require very many years of intensive study in order to acquire the depth and breadth of knowledge necessary to understand how Torah law relates to many complex issues in contemporary life. In the majority of cases, candidates for the rabbinate can finance their studies only through support from others.

Similarly, the service of HaShem by the Gentile Nations requires not only the pursuit of the study and practice of the Seven Universal Commandments by all people, but also trained, competent professionals who can conduct classes for children, teenagers and adults, conduct worship and life-cycle events (birth and naming, coming of age, marriage and divorce, illness, death), counseling, public speaking, public relations and outreach online, in print, TV and radio etc.

The only way that Jewish and Gentile groups and communities can ensure that they will receive the Torah teaching, guidance and leadership they vitally need is through paying the necessary price for Torah professionalism and expertise, just as they pay for it in medicine, law, business, education and science. "If there is no flour, there is no Torah" (Avot 3:17).

The Priestly Garments

Only the High Priest when serving in the Temple wore the glorious gold, blue, scarlet, purple, bejeweled vestments described in our present Torah portion. This is because of the unique role which the Torah accords to the High Priest in securing atonement for Israel and the whole world, and every detail of each of his garments, worn for the glory of God, is replete with deep morals and lessons.

But all the other priests without exception wore the identical simple white linen trousers, tunics, belts and hats described in Exodus chapter 28 verses 40 and 42 when serving in the Temple. There was no place there for gorgeous arrays of human finery of diverse kinds that magnify the wearers each according to his level in some hierarchy. In the Temple of HaShem, only the High Priest, His chosen minister, wears the golden vestments for His glory; all the other Cohanim have the simplest uniforms as His humble servants.

This teaches that the Cohen was not intended to live a life of magnificent luxury and splendor but one of simple, humble service and devotion to the study and practice of God's Torah.

No-one but the son of a Cohen can be a Cohen. But everyone in the world, Gentile or Israelite, can try to emulate the true Cohen's calling of simplicity, humility and devotion in the service of HaShem.

Idolatry and the Power of Repentance

Our portion tells the story of the sin of the golden calf, which took place only forty days after all Israel stood at Mt Sinai in awe and trembling to hear God's solemn injunction:

"You shall have no other gods before Me. You shall not make for yourself a graven image or any kind of likeness of any thing that is in heaven above or that is in the earth beneath or that is in the water under the earth; you shall not bow down to them or serve them..." (Exodus 20:3).

This is the second of the Ten Commandments. After all the people heard them, Moses ascended Mt Sinai for forty to receive all the details of the Torah code, while the people awaited his return in order to lead them up from the wilderness to the Promised Land. But when the expected moment of Moses' reappearance passed, the people feared he was lost forever and set themselves to make a visible "god" that would lead them:

"And when the people saw that Moses delayed coming down from the mount, the people gathered together with Aaron and said to him: 'Get up and make us a god who shall go before us; for as for this Moses, the man that brought us up out of the land of Egypt, we do not know what has become of him.' Aaron said to them: 'Break off the golden rings in the ears of your wives, sons and daughters and bring them to me.' ... And he received it from their hand and fashioned it with a sculpting tool and made it a molten calf. And they said: 'These are your gods, O Israel, which brought you up out of the land of Egypt.' ... And they rose up early the next day and offered burnt-offerings, and peace-offerings; and the people sat down to eat and to drink, and rose up to make merry" (Exodus 30: 1-6).

The Torah sages taught that this "merry-making" included the murder of any opponents as well as the embrace of complete sexual license (see Rashi on Exodus 30:6 and Genesis 21:9). Thus idolatry led the people to the very opposite of the Torah path they had been commanded.

How was it possible for people who had witnessed God's revelation of His absolute unity and sovereignty to fall to these depths only forty days later?

Rabbi Shimon bar Yochai, author of the Zohar, taught that there was a divine necessity in Israel's fall and subsequent repentance, because in and of themselves they should not have sinned since God Himself testified that at the time when they accepted Torah at Sinai they had true fear of God (Deuteronomy 5:26). If they sinned, it came to teach the entire world that it is possible to repent -

for as soon as Moses did return and showed them the gravity of their sin, they repented. And in future, if any community would err into idolatry, we can say to them: Go and learn from Israel that even after a sin, it is always possible to repent (Talmud Bavli, Avodah Zarah 4b).

What is idolatry?

We all need to understand what is considered to be idolatry since it is prohibited in the second of the Ten Commandments heard by Israel at Sinai (Exodus 20:3, quoted above), and also under the first of the Seven Noahide Laws, which apply to all humanity.

The prohibition of idolatry has two aspects: (1) It is prohibited to serve and worship any power less than the Absolute One God - HaShem; (2) It is forbidden to use statues or graven image of any creature in the service of HaShem, let alone in the service of some subordinate power. Violation of either of these aspects impugns the absolute unity and sovereignty of God.

The Unity of God

Moses Maimonides writes in the opening words of his comprehensive compendium of Torah law:

"The foundation of all foundations... is to know that there exists the First Existent, and He brought into being all that exists, and all the existents in the heavens and on earth and all that is in between exist only in virtue of His existence. This Existent is the God of the World and Lord of all the Earth, and He runs the cycle with a power that has no end or limit, with a power that is never interrupted, so that the cycle turns continuously. It is impossible that it could turn without one turning it, and He, blessed be He, is the One that turns it without a hand and without a body...

"This God is one and not two or more than two but one in a way to which no other unity is comparable, neither the unity of one of the entities that exist in the world nor a unity that comprises numerous entities together, nor a unity such as that of the body, which is divided into different sections and limbs, but a unity such that there is no other unity in the world to compare with it" (Mishneh Torah, Foundations of the Torah, 1:1).

Prohibition of graven images

Since God's absolute unity and sovereignty are totally beyond the comprehension of the human mind, it is strictly forbidden to use images of entities in this world to try to conceive of Him, let alone to worship subordinate entities and to use images in their service, because this necessarily detracts from God's supremacy.

Thus Moses warned Israel: "Therefore take good care of yourselves - for you saw no kind of form on the day that HaShem spoke to you in Horeb out of the midst of the fire, lest you deal corruptly and make for yourself a graven image, the form of any figure, the likeness of male or female, the likeness of any beast that is on the earth, the likeness of any winged fowl that flies in the heaven, the likeness of any thing that creeps on the ground, the likeness of any fish that is in the water under the earth; and lest you lift up your eyes to heaven, and when you see the sun and the moon and the stars - all the host of heaven - you be drawn away and worship them and serve them." (Deuteronomy 4:15-19).

Maimonides' defines idolatry as follows: "The essential commandment against idolatry prohibits worshipping any one of all the creations - not an angel nor a sphere nor a star nor one of the four elements ("fire", "water", "spirit" or "earth") nor any one of all the beings created out of them. And even though the worshipper knows that HaShem is the God and intends to serve this created being in the way that Enosh and his generation worshipped [the stars as if to give honor to God's ministers] this is idolatry..." (Maimonides, Laws of Idolatry 2:1).

The penalty for idolatry

The Torah lays down very severe penalties for idolatry:

"Every person who worships idols willfully and flag-rantly is liable to spiritual excision, and if witnesses were present and he received due warning, he is executed through stoning, while if he worshipped unwittingly he must bring a fixed sin offering" (ibid 3:1).

However these penalties may not be imposed without due legal process, and in the absence of the Temple in Jerusalem and the Sanhedrin (Court of the Sages) on the Temple Mount, no court of law in the world is competent to inflict them, let alone the self-appointed "religious police" who take the law into their own hands to punish supposed idolaters, as in the case of the various radical terrorists who justify indiscriminate terror outrages against masses of innocent men, women and children on the grounds that the terrorists and their handlers deem these victims guilty of supposed idolatry. Only a duly constituted Torah court can determine what is or is not idolatry, and even in cases of suspected idolatry, all due processes of law must be fulfilled (cf. Rambam Laws of Idolatry 4:5-6).

It is easy to see that clear-cut cases of polytheistic religious worship involving the use of statues and other images of the deities (as in ancient Greece and Rome) contravene the Torah prohibition of idolatry. However, it can be far more problematic to determine if certain practices in the so-called monotheistic religions are to be considered idolatrous or not under Torah law.

Certain forms of Christianity seemingly involve the worship of the Godhead through different personae, yet elaborate theologies explain that they are all one: is this idolatry? Some Christians use statues and images in their rituals, yet they claim that the object of worship is not the statue or image itself, which functions only to direct the mind to God. Are Buddhist statues idolatrous? Are Hindu statues idolatrous? Is the veneration of the Temple Mount in Jerusalem or the Kaaba in Mecca or the grave of some saint or righteous person idolatrous? Is having pictures of saints or other inspiring figures around the house idolatrous? What about pictures of film stars and sports heroes...?

Serving an intermediary

The story of the Golden Calf teaches that the essence of idolatry is the veneration of some subsidiary force or power in itself in place of the worship and service of the One God. Under this definition, idolatry may often be far subtler than the mere crude worship of statues of wood and stone, gold and silver.

Thus for some people the intermediary to whom they look for security, help and support is their wealth and assets, accumulated through the work of their hands. "Their idols are silver and gold, the work of the hands of man" (Psalms 115:4). Sometimes sick people and those around them behave as if they believe that the doctors and their medicines are the gods. The terrorist looks to his machine gun and explosives as his gods and source of power.

In the words of Rabbi Nachman of Breslov:

"Many people make the mistake of turning the means through which something comes about into an intermediary between themselves and God. They do believe in God, but they also believe in the intermediary, saying that we have no option but to depend upon a particular means in order to bring about a certain result. For example, they put their faith in their business activities as the cause of their livelihood, placing all the emphasis on their own endeavors as if God would somehow not be able to provide their livelihood without them. Likewise people put all the emphasis on the means through which a cure comes about - the medicine - as if without medicine God does not have the power to heal. That is not so. The Holy One, blessed be He, is the Cause of all causes, and there is absolutely no need for any one particular means. **Even while resorting to a given means to try to bring something about, we must believe only in God, and not put our faith in the means** (Likutey Moharan I, 62).

We need to understand the laws of idolatry not in order to impose the death penalty on those who think and behave differently from the way we do, but rather so that we ourselves may learn to avoid the subtle forms of idolatry of which we ourselves may be guilty, and so that we may encourage others to understand where they are in error in order to help them to repent.

When Israel sincerely repented of the sin of making the Golden Calf, God forgave them. This makes it easier for all who have sinned after them to repent.

Treasures and Transparency

The last two portions of the Book of Exodus, known after their Hebrew opening words as **Vayakhel**, "And [Moses] assembled", and **Pekudey**, "[These are the] Accounts", are in some years read in the synagogue on separate Sabbaths, while in others they are read together on the same Sabbath. (This depends on how the Torah calendar reconciles the lunar months with the annual solar cycle in different years.)

Previously we learned about the design of the wilderness Sanctuary which God instructed Moses to make (Terumah, Exodus 25:1-27:19) and the design of the priests' garments and how their ceremonial induction was to be conducted (Tetzaveh, Exodus 27:20-30:10). Now in **Vayakhel** and **Pekudey** we are shown how Moses led the children of Israel in the execution of this great collective national enterprise in the actual material world. We learn how the people donated the various materials and how the skilled craftsmen prepared all the components, culminating in the erection of the Sanctuary at the foot of Mount Sinai and its consecration on the first day of the month of Nissan, one year after the Exodus from Egypt.

VAYAKHEL
Treasures: Each makes a unique contribution

All whose hearts aroused them and all whose spirits made them willing came and brought HaShem's offering for the work of the tent of meeting, and for all its service, and for the holy garments. And they came, both men and women, as many as were willing-hearted, and brought nose-rings, ear-rings, signet-rings, girdles, all jewels of gold. And everyone who had blue, purple and scarlet dyed wool and fine linen, goats' hair, rams' skins dyed red and sealskins brought them. Everyone that set aside an offering of silver and brass brought HaShem's offering; and everyone who had acacia-wood for any work of the service, brought it ... The children of Israel brought a freewill-offering to HaShem; every man and woman whose heart made them willing to bring for all the work which HaShem had commanded through the hand of Moses to be made (Exodus 35:21-24, 29).

The various different physical materials that different men and women had in their possession and contributed for the construction of the Sanctuary correspond to the unique personal attributes and powers possessed by each and every individual.

Moses' call to all the people - the men and the women - was for each and every one to discover and understand his or her own unique personal treasures, skills and abilities and to contribute them for the glorification of God through His chosen Sanctuary, so as to bring harmony and peace into all creation.

The later Chassidic sage Rabbi Nachman of Breslov (1772-1810) called these personal treasures one's "good points", urging us to search after the redeeming good attributes each one of us possesses so as to know how we can make our own contribution to bless God's creation through our efforts in this life.

These "good points" are not to be understood as static attributes but rather as dynamic "power points" that bring us to perform practical **actions** in the real material world so as to make our own individual contributions to bring about God's greater purpose.

In the present age more than ever before we live in a world of enormously complex organizations involving intense specialization at all levels of society, in industry and commerce, education, communications and most other spheres of life, such that every person has his or her unique contribution to make.

So too in the spiritual sphere each has a unique role in constructing the great Temple that is constructed out of each and every person's unique good deeds, prayers and even the simplest acts and gestures of virtue for the sake of God. Much of the good that righteous people do may go unseen by the eyes of flesh and blood and unreported in the media, but God knows and registers everything, and no good thought, word or deed is ever lost.

In the words of the Mishnaic sage Ben Azai: "Do not be scornful of any person and do not be disdainful of anything, for you have no person without his hour and nothing without its place" (Avot 2:3).

PEKUDEY
Transparency

The portion of **Pekudey** opens with a detailed and exact accounting of the various materials which the people contributed for the different parts of the Sanctuary, and what was done with their contributions:

These are the accounts of the tabernacle - the tabernacle of the testimony - as they were rendered according to the commandment of Moses through the service of the Levites, by the hand of Ithamar, the son of Aaron the priest:

All the gold that was used for the work in all the work of the sanctuary, the gold of the offering, was twenty nine talents, and seven hundred and thirty shekels according to the Sanctuary standard shekel. And the silver of those of the community that were numbered was a hundred talents, and one thousand seven hundred and seventy-five shekels, according to the Sanctuary standard shekel. And from the blue, and purple, and scarlet dyed wool they made plaited garments for ministering in the holy place, and they made holy garments for Aaron, as HaShem commanded Moses... (Exodus 38: 21-25, 39:1).

Theocratic societies are often ruled by priestly castes, all access to whose secret lore and inner workings is strictly sealed off from the general public. The same could be said to apply today under most governments, religious or secular, monarchical or "democratic", throughout the world.

The book of Exodus concludes with Moses' lesson in **transparent government**. Having imposed a "tax" of the silver half-shekel and invited voluntary contributions of other materials for the Sanctuary, Moses gives a complete accounting of all that was received and exactly what was done with it. Everything was conducted under the eye of full public scrutiny with no cover-ups, scams or filching from ordinary people's contributions for private use and other forms of corruption. Everything is open, honest and laid upon the table for all to see.

Likewise the entire Torah is open to the eyes of all men and women anywhere in the world. Through the Internet anyone can find out how to acquire Torah texts. If they are capable of learning Hebrew and Aramaic and studying the original sources, they will be able to see for themselves that everything in this book **Torah for the Nations** is based on the authentic foundations of HaShem's Torah as received through the hand of Moses at

Mount Sinai as expounded by the sages of Israel in the Mishnah, Talmud, Codes, Kabbalah and Chassidut.

Many translations of the authoritative sources have been made into various languages making the Torah accessible to all. Yet she reveals and uncovers the many secret treasures buried deep in her words and letters, crowns and melodies only to those who seek out her wisdom more earnestly than people seek gold and silver.

To understand the in-depth meaning of the Torah depends upon two foundations that are secret in the heart of each and every person: Love of God and Fear of God. Only you and I - and God Himself - know in our own hearts if we have true Love and Fear of God. It is upon these two hidden foundations that the entire edifice stands.

Sacrifices

The book of Exodus concluded with the account of the completion of the Sanctuary, or "Tent of Meeting". Directly following, Leviticus opens with God's call to Moses from the Sanctuary, just as He had promised:

"And there I will meet with you, and I will speak with you from above the ark-cover, from between the two cherubim which are upon the ark of the testimony, about all that I will command you for the children of Israel" (Exodus 25:22).

Prior to the construction of the Sanctuary the Torah had emanated from Mount Sinai, but once it was erected, all revelation of the Torah came forth from this Tent of Meeting - where God meets man and man meets God. While many different laws were later given to Moses from this Sanctuary, the very first were the laws of the services of the Temple itself and how they were to be conducted by its "officers" - the Cohanim (Priests).

Sacrifice

The concept of sacrifice - a "gift" of some kind that a person offers to God - appears very early in the Torah:

"And Abel was a shepherd of flocks while Cain worked the land. And after a period of time Cain brought from the fruits of the earth as an offering to God. And Abel also brought from the first-born of his flocks and from their fat, and God showed favor to Abel and to his offering" (Genesis 4:2-4).

All the various offerings described in our present portion are likewise either from living creatures (oxen, sheep, goats, doves and pigeons) or from the fruits of the earth (wheat, barley, olive oil and grape wine).

In modern times everyone admires those who "sacrifice" their own selves and personal resources for some greater cause or purpose. However the pouring of libations and burning of grain flour, loaves and wafers etc. on an altar is widely seen as primitive, while slitting an animal's throat, sprinkling its blood and burning its fat and limbs on the altar would be considered quite barbaric by many - though most of them have no qualms about the sacrifice of barbeque and other meats down people's gullets for the sake of human gratification. Even so, there is a widespread tendency to view religious blood sacrifices and burnt offerings as a pagan method of trying to propitiate angry gods in order to elicit their help and protection. Many would be highly resistant to the idea that the Temple sacrifices as set forth in our portion should be reinstated.

Yet whether they like it or not, the Temple services will indeed be reinstated by King Messiah, as stated clearly in the conclusion of the comprehensive *Mishneh Torah* Law Code of Moses Maimonides (Rambam): "King Messiah is destined to arise and restore the kingship of David to its original glory and he will build the Temple and gather the scattered of Israel and all the laws will be restored in his days as they were originally: **they will offer the sacrifices** and practice the Sabbatical and Jubilee years, and everyone who does not believe in him or does not wait for his coming not only denies the other prophets but the very Torah itself and Moses our Teacher" (Laws of Kings 11:1).

Those who refuse to accept that the Temple sacrifices will be restored will either not be there to see them, or will be forced to bow to the higher wisdom of the Torah and seek to understand why it prescribes the **korban**. This Hebrew term is normally translated into English with the word "sacrifice" but its true meaning is impossible to render in a single English word. **Korban** derives from the Hebrew root **karov**, "near", and signifies that the offering brings the creations of this world - people, other living creatures, trees and plants and even the mineral world - **nearer** and **closer** to their divine roots.

Some of the offerings described in our portion are to be brought daily or on Sabbaths and festivals and at various other junctures on behalf of the entire people of Israel through their represen-tatives - the priests. The purpose is to accomplish certain spiritual repairs required by Israel, by the other peoples of the world, animal, vegetable and mineral creations, angels and other spiritual levels, as discussed in the Torah mystical texts. Other offerings are prescribed for individuals to entrust to the Cohanim for sacrifice either as freewill gifts or to atone for certain sins.

Atonement for sin does not come about automatically and vicariously through the killing of the animal. Without repentance and prayer on the part of the sinner, the animal sacrifice accomplishes nothing. In the words of Maimonides: "When people bring sin and guilt offerings whether for unwitting or willful offenses, no atonement is given to them through their offering until they actively repent and make verbal confession, as it is written, 'And he shall confess over it the sin he committed'" (Leviticus 5:5; Rambam, Laws of Repentance 1:1). Immediately prior to the slaughter of the animal, the sinner had to place his two hands upon it and pour out his heart in grief and contrition over his sin (see Rambam, Sacrificial Procedure 3:14). He would then witness the terrifying spectacle of the animal having its throat cut and being flayed, cut to pieces and burned on the altar, plunging him into humility and broken-heartedness. The service requires the utmost intense concentration and all the correct intentions on the part of the priests, or else the sacrifice is invalid.

Categories of Sacrifice:

Our portion sets forth the four main categories of sacrifices brought in the Temple by the Children of Israel:

1. Olah, literally "rising up", often translated as a "whole-burnt-offering" because not only was the animal's blood sprinkled on the Altar but all its fat and limbs were burned thereon. The Olah offering might be an ox, sheep, goat, dove or pigeon, or grain flour, loaves or wafers.

2. Shelamim, "peace offerings", where the blood and fat went on the Altar, but all the portions of the meat were consumed by the Cohen, the person offering the sacrifice and his guests.

3. Chat'at, sin offerings, where the blood and animal fat were burned on the Altar while the meat was eaten ceremonially by the priests in the Temple precincts.

4. Asham, guilt-offerings for certain specified sins or certain cases of doubt if one had sinned. Like the Chat'at sin offerings, blood and fats of the Asham guilt offerings were offered on the Altar while the priests ate the portions.

Sacrifices by Gentiles in the Temple

Our portion is specifically addressed to Children of Israel: God's opening words to Moses from the Sanctuary were: "Speak to the **Children of Israel** and say to them: when a man from among you offers a Korban to God." (Leviticus 1:2).

Is there a place for offerings in the Temple by Gentiles? The answer is Yes, as Maimonides states: "From gentiles only Olah burnt offerings are accepted. even an Olah offering of a bird may be accepted from a gentile even if he worships idols, but neither Shelamim peace offerings nor meal offerings nor sin or guilt sacrifices are accepted from them. If an Israelite reverted to idolatry or publicly desecrates the Sabbath, no sacrifice whatever is accepted from him: not even the Olah offering that can be accepted from the gentiles is accepted from this renegade." (Laws of Sacrificial Procedure 3:2-4).

Sacrifices by Gentiles outside the Temple:

A significant difference between the people of Israel and the Gentiles is that since the inauguration of King Solomon's Temple in Jerusalem, Israel are strictly forbidden to sacrifice anywhere except on Mount Moriah (Maimonides, Laws of the Temple, 1:3). The gentiles, on the other hand, are permitted to bring sacrifices in any suitable place anywhere in the world.

"Gentiles are permitted to offer burnt offerings to God in all places on condition that they offer it on a Bamah-altar which they build. It is forbidden [for an Israelite] to assist them since we are forbidden to bring offerings outside [Jerusalem], but it is permitted to instruct them and teach them how to make offerings to for the sake of God, blessed be He" (Maimonides, Laws of Sacrificial Procedure 19:16).

To begin to grasp the purpose of the Torah sacrificial system requires earnest prayer to God for enlightenment. The external ritual comes to break the inner human heart, until we are truly willing to sacrifice and submit our ego and head-strong will to God.

"For You do not delight in sacrifice, or else would I give it; You have no pleasure in burnt-offering. The sacrifices of G-d are a broken spirit; a broken and a contrite heart, O God, You will not despise" (Psalms 51:18-19).

Thank You!

Our portion continues to fill in the details of the various procedures for Temple offerings in each of the four main categories of sacrifices: the whole-burnt (olah), meal (minchah), sin (chatat), guilt (asham) and peace (shelamim) offerings. One particular kind of peace offering is the Thanks-giving Offering:

"And this is the law of the sacrifice of peace-offerings which one may offer to HaShem. If he offers it for a thanksgiving." (Leviticus 7:11).

It is striking that the Torah introduces the portion about the thanksgiving offering with the word **if**. This implies that making an offering as an expression of gratitude to God is not an absolute obligation that the Torah imposes upon us. Rather it is a voluntary act that we carry out because we have become aware of His goodness and kindness to us through His many miracles, and we seek some way to acknowledge Him.

In Temple times Israelites would bring the thanksgiving offering specified in our portion (Lev. 7:11-15) for one of four kinds of miraculous deliverance enumerated in the lengthy psalm of thanksgiving in Psalms 107: deliverance from being lost in the wilderness (Ps. 107, vv. 4-9), held in captivity (vv. 10-16), sick with a dangerous illness (vv. 17-22) and threatened with shipwreck (vv. 23-32).

"Give thanks to HaShem for He is good, for His mercy endures forever. So let the redeemed of HaShem say. Let them give thanks to HaShem for His mercy, and for His wonderful works to the children of men! Let them exalt Him also in the assembly of the people, and praise Him in the seat of the elders" (Psalms 107, vv. 31-32).

It is deeply humbling to experience an amazing rescue from a critical life-threatening situation, knowing that one's life was hanging by a thread and was snatched from the claws of death only by a fluke event. The proper response is to reflect on how this fluke can only be a sign of how God is invisibly watching over us constantly, protecting us with loving care. What could we possibly "give" to God in return for such kindness if not our thanks? In the case of very striking miracles, the bene-ficiaries should give their thanks publicly "in the assembly of the people and. in the seat of the elders" - for telling the story of the miracle to many others provides a graphic illustration of the wonders of God's ways, strengthening their faith.

Great miracles may not be visible every day. We live in a world governed by the regularities of nature: gravity pulls everything down to earth; the sun rises, passes over and sets; earth's tilted orbit causes hot weather in summer and cold in winter;

the rains fall, the plants grow, the animals and humans eat and get fat, the factories produce, electricity makes all the gadgets work. We are born, live our lives and die.

The deeper we reflect, the more we may see how the multitude of natural laws and processes that govern the world are in themselves totally amazing, and the complex, subtle ways in which they interact to create all the manifold details of the creation in general and in the personal life of each and every one of us is itself an expression of God's kindness and mercy to all.

Thinking about the many kindnesses God has shown one personally and giving thanks to Him for them is the first step towards deeper knowledge and understanding of His ways - for while God intrinsically is unknowable, His dealings with each and every one are signs and indications of His unceasing watchful presence.

Before asking God for what one needs, one should first start counting and reflecting upon some of His many goodnesses to us so far, such as the miracles of our bodily functioning, health, vision, hearing, taste, smell, touch, the fact that we have survived all the years and all the vicissitudes, eaten and enjoyed many benefits and blessings. In the words of Rabbi Nachman: "When a person wants to pray to God and ask for what he needs, he should first thank God for all of His past kindnesses and only then ask for what he needs. Because if he starts by asking only for what he needs, God says, 'Have you nothing to thank Me for then?'" (Siach Sarfey Kodesh 1-2).

We may be disappointed with certain aspects of our lives or think ourselves to be in desperate need of certain things we feel we lack. Yet if we are willing to examine negative aspects of our lives in the wider context of other positive aspects, we may come to understand that even the negative stems from God's watchful care. Again, in the words of Rabbi Nachman: "When a person knows that everything that happens to him is for his own good, this is a foretaste of the world to come. To be serene and patient regardless of what you encounter in life is the highest level of knowledge and understanding of God. Have faith that everything is for your ultimate good" (Likutey Moharan I, 4).

Giving thanks to God for His visible kindnesses to us leads us to deeper humility before Him, enabling us to acknowledge the negative within ourselves, to seek to rectify it, and to accept in faith the wisdom of His inscrutable dealings with us through all that He has sent us in our lives. "For His mercy endures forever!"

"I will not reprove you for your sacrifices; and your burnt-offerings are continually before Me. I will take no bullock out of your house, nor he-goats out of your pens. For every beast of the forest is Mine, and the cattle upon a thousand hills. I know all the birds of the mountains, and the wild beasts of the field are Mine. If I were hungry, I would not tell you; for the world is Mine and its fullness. Do I eat the meat of bulls, or drink the blood of goats? Offer to God the sacrifice of thanksgiving and pay your vows to the Most High. And call upon Me on the day of trouble; I will deliver you, and you shall honor Me... Whoever offers the sacrifice of thanksgiving honors Me; and to the person that orders his way right I will show the salvation of G-d" (Psalms 50: 8-15; 23).

Sober Judgment

Our portion tells the chilling story of the disaster that struck on the very day of one of the great summits of human history: the inauguration of the proto-Temple Sanctuary in the wilderness by Moses and Aaron.

"And Nadav and Avihu, the sons of Aaron, each took his censer, and put fire in it and laid incense upon it, and offered strange fire before God, which He had not commanded them. And a fire came forth from before God and devoured them, and they died before God" (Leviticus 10:1-2).

The two crown princes of the priestly line of Aaron the High Priest had no children, and thus were extirpated in a moment. Directly after this terrible decree, God commanded Aaron:

"Drink no wine or strong drink, you and your surviving sons, when you enter the Tent of Meeting, in order that you should not die. And so that you may distinguish between the holy and the ordinary, and between the unclean and the clean; so that you may teach the Children of Israel all the statutes which God has told them through the hand of Moses." (Lev. 9:10-11).

The simple implication of the text is that the reason why Nadab and Abihu incurred this severest of penalties was because they were intoxicated when they made their offering. Wine or some other strong substance distorted their faculty of proper judgment, causing them to err gravely in determining what service God wanted from them. They offered "strange fire", eliciting God's consuming fire to destroy them.

The priests are the spiritual leaders of the community, with two main functions: (1) To offer the people's sacrifices (leadership in the aspect of prayer, our offerings to God); (2) To educate the people in God's Torah (the teachings God gives to us). Both functions involve intense concentration of the spiritual leaders' mental and all other faculties to ensure proper balanced focus on the task in hand, be it leading the people in prayer and devotion or providing sound guidance and true judgment.

Wine and other intoxicating substances simply interfere with a person's normal rational thinking and functioning, and can take them into delirious flights of fancy where they may be absolutely convinced that they are perfectly sane and focused. The first case of such intoxication in the Bible, which likewise had the severest consequences, was that of Noah, father of humanity, as told in Genesis 9:20-27. Clear understanding of the Torah view of intoxication is important to all people.

Physical substances

"Wine rejoices the heart of man" (Psalms 104:15): God has created wine and other varieties of amazing life-enhancers - including even coffee, tea and other herbs etc. - that when properly used in moderation at appropriate times may help temporarily lift the human heart out of the cyclical heaviness and depression to which so many are prone. There may be a place for some of the life-enhancing substances that exist in creation. But when it comes to our spiritual affairs - our prayers to God, our study of His Torah - and particularly when community leaders and governments must pass judgments on proper laws and their applications in actual life situations - the state of mind that is required is one of sobriety, level-headedness and clear judgment.

Mental poisons

This level-headedness is liable to be distorted not only by physical mind-changing substances but also by various kinds of insidious false beliefs that act as intoxicants which drive arrogant madmen and fanatics to justify and perpetrate murder, cruel abuse and other crimes against God and man through terrible errors of judgment.

The exact determination of what God wants of man depends upon exact interpretation of the Torah text and authentic traditions. The application of the law in actual cases requires the ability to make sense of many conflicting testimonies, claims and counterclaims based on people's divergent outlooks and worldviews and their accompanying narratives.

When making any kind of judgments about situations that are unclear, the common tendency is to liken elements in the situation to things that we are clear about. For example, we know that murder, theft and oppression are wrong. If we need to pass a judgment or make our own personal evaluation about a people or country accused of such crimes, we need to make a careful evaluation of all the arguments and evidence of all sides.

Slander

But just as on a dark night, a drunkard or drug-taker or even simply a frightened child may see a terrifying ogre lurching towards them when all that stands there is a great tree, likewise those who are intoxicated by false beliefs fueled by lies and slanders may see a given group, people or country as a terrible ogre when the truth is nothing of the kind.

Today's sophisticated mass media, concentrated in the hands of the world's power barons, are masters of the art of mental manipulation through spinning all their output and "information" in their own desired direction. All over the world in different ways, disinformation, subtle smears and slanders enter and intoxicate people's minds, attitudes and opinions, leading them in directions that are putting the future of humanity in dire peril.

One of the most widespread forms of distorted thinking resulting from the mental intoxication caused by poisonous lies and slanders is the kind of reasoning that says: "Mr. X committed a crime; Mr. X is a Teuton. Therefore, all Teutons must be criminals." It is false deductions of this kind that historically have led to every kind of intergroup hatred and strife until today.

The grim story of the extirpation of Nadav and Avihu, sons of Aaron the High Priest, through intoxication teaches the extreme care needed to keep our mental faculties intact and balanced in life situations that require focus and clear judgment. Not only must dangerous mind-changing substances be rejected completely, but so must mind-shackling poisonous lies and slanders that have no less a power to lead people to the worst kinds of destruction.

Evil Speech

Each of the two portions that are the subject of today's commentary is considered a separate portion in its own right in the annual cycle of the fifty-three weekly portions of the Five Books of Moses. In some years each of these two is read on its own Sabbath. However, in many years the Jewish lunar calendar requires the reading of both together, one after the other, on one and the same Sabbath (as happens in the case of a number of other "double" portions). The twinning of **Tazria** and **Metzora** is particularly justified since both are mainly devoted to the subject of **Tzora'at**, "Biblical" leprosy.

I am calling **Tzora'at** "Biblical" leprosy in order to distinguish this collective term for various kinds of morbid marks and patches that may appear on the skin, head, garments of wool or linen and even stone walls of houses from what today is normally considered "leprosy" i.e. Hansen's disease (so-named after the German physician Gerhard Henrik Armauer Hansen, 1841-1912), which if left untreated can cause permanent disfigurement and damage to the skin, nerves, limbs and eyes.

The external marks of Hansen's kind of leprosy on the head and body may or may not relate to those delineated in our portions as one of the main kinds of **Tzora'at** as it afflicts the human body. This leads to the shunning of the leper as ritually impure, and he is literally cast out of the town. However, the fact that **Tzora'at** may also take hold of a garment or the walls of houses indicates that the Biblical concept encompasses more kinds of afflictions than Hansen's disease alone.

In the rabbinic tradition **Tzora'at** is seen as a Heaven-sent chastisement and a wake-up call to certain categories of sinners, in particular to one who is guilty of saying evil things about other people. At first the chastisement may manifest as a disturbing morbid bright red or green "mould" growing on a garment. If the sinner fails to repent so as to cause the growth to disappear, the next wake-up call may be sent to the very stone blocks of his house. The infected stones have to be ripped out in full public view and buried away from the town. If the person still does not repent, the feared patches of infected, lifeless or discolored skin may appear on his or her very head and body with all the accompanying embarrassment and social ostracization. The disfiguring blemishes that appear all over the **metzora** ("leper") are a punishment, measure for measure, for his or her incessant disparagement and slander of other people. Now his or her own blemishes are horribly visible for all to see. Thus, the Hebrew word **metzora** has the same Hebrew consonant-letters as the words **motzi-ra**, which mean "one that brings forth evil", i.e. from his or her mouth in the form of evil speech.

The specific Biblical prohibition of evil speech is contained not in either of our present portions but later on in Leviticus 19:16: "Do not go around telling tales among your people..." It is also forbidden to accept slander (Exodus 23:1). The severity of the prohibition of evil speech is vividly illustrated in the case of Moses' older sister Miriam, who for a very minor infringement was immediately stricken with leprosy (Numbers 12:1). In order to inculcate in us a strong awareness of how terrible is the sin of evil speech, the Torah commands us to remember constantly how even the righteous Miriam was stricken because of her inappropriate words (Deuteronomy 24:9).

Evil speech is part of a nexus of interrelated sins in the way we humans may use our all-important faculty of speech - the gift that distinguishes us from all other species - for "death and life are in the hands of the tongue". The ultimate purpose of speech is for us to communicate and share words of truth, so that all humans will learn to call on the Name of One with one accord (Zephaniah 3:9). Among the various ways people may abuse their gift of speech, are:

Telling lies;

Bearing false witness;

Swearing false oaths;

Taking vows and making verbal undertakings, then violating or failing to fulfill them;

Talking directly to others in ways that are hurtful and insulting;

Talking **about** others - whether they are present or not - in ways that are disparaging and potentially harmful to them, even when what is said is **true**!

It is permissible to tell someone in a discreet manner about flaws and criticisms relating to a particular person or persons, their behavior and traits etc. when this may be of benefit to the person in question or necessary for the welfare of others (as when confidentially providing someone with information they need in order to make a wise decision about a possible purchase, prospective partner, placement etc. in business or other areas of life).

What is specifically forbidden is the kind of malicious gossip about everyone and anyone that today knows no boundaries not only among family, friends and various social groups but particularly in the public arenas of politics, entertainment and the mass media.

The first to bring Evil Speech into the world was the primordial serpent, who cast aspersions on God Himself in contradicting His explicit warning to

Adam and Eve not to eat from the Tree of Knowledge, accusing Him of being jealous of His creatures (Genesis 3:1-5).

Casting aspersions on other people through various kinds of unduly harsh judgments, criticism, disparaging remarks, slurs and slanders etc. is itself disparaging to God, since they are His creatures and His way is to judge everyone with kindness and mercy.

In the contemporary world the ancient subtle craft of the serpent is practiced with exceptional skill by the TV, radio, newspapers and magazines and via the Internet, where the trials of all kinds of people ranging from suspected criminals to the most prominent celebrities, politicians, entertainers, sportsmen, other personalities, groups and even entire peoples and countries are conducted by slick media presenters through innuendoes and telling images and snippets of out-of-context footage without judge or jury or any possibility of appeal, fanning the flames of resentment, hatred and war.

Perhaps some kind of contemporary manifestation of **tzora'at** and other chastisements from heaven are visible in the mysterious ecological plagues and blights that afflict our vegetation, wildlife, livestock etc., the strange afflictions of various structures, buildings and private homes with all manner of faulty installations, and particularly the terrible chronic health problems and diseases that afflict so many, young and old, in our communities.

The outstanding modern rabbinic authority Rabbi Yisrael Meir Kagan (1838-1933), known popularly as the Chofetz Chaim (Lover of Life) from the words in Psalms 34:13, saw the sin of evil speech - malicious gossip and slander - as the worst sin of the present era, and he wrote guides to the rules of permitted and forbidden speech, emphasizing the great benefits that come from speaking properly and the terrible evils that stem from the opposite. For "he who guards his mouth guards his soul" (Proverbs 13:3).

The Greatest Love

The two consecutive Torah portions known respectively by their Hebrew names of **Acharey Mot** and **Kedoshim** are in some years read each on their own separate Shabbat, while in other years they may be read together on the same Shabbat, according to the requirements of the Jewish lunar calendar (as discussed in the portion).

Moral Purity

Each of these two portions has its own unique content, but they also contain the shared theme of moral purity, one of whose chief foundations lies in the observance of certain basic incest prohibitions that apply in all human societies. The concluding section of **Acharey Mot** (Leviticus chapter 18) sets forth the various kinds of incestuous unions that are forbidden specifically to the Children of Israel, while the concluding section of **Kedoshim** (Leviticus chapter 20) sets forth the specific Biblical punishments for violating those prohibitions.

The incest prohibitions that apply to all humanity under the Noahide code are set forth by Rabbi Moses Maimonides ("Rambam" 1137-1204) in his comprehensive Torah code (Mishneh Torah, Laws of Kings 9:5). They are: relations between a son and his mother or his father's wife or with any woman that is married to another man, with his maternal sister, with a transvestite, and bestiality.

Violation of these fundamental prohibitions may lead to many evils both for their practitioners and for the wider society, while the observance and practice of God's fundamental statutes for humankind brings to the greatest good.

Introducing the list of Torah incest prohibitions, God says:

"And you shall guard My statutes and My laws which, when a man (Hebrew: Adam) does them, he shall **live** through them, **I am Hashem**" (Leviticus 18:5).

In commenting on this verse, the most ancient rabbinic midrashic commentary on Leviticus, **Sifra Devey Rav**, goes to some lengths to prove that this applies to all mankind. "It does not say 'which, when a Cohen or Levi or Israelite does them' but 'when a **man**-- HaAdam -- does them', including a **Gentile**".

Love your neighbor

"Sandwiched" in between the list of incest prohibitions (Leviticus 18:6-29) and the list of their penalties (Leviticus 20:1-27) is the beautiful lengthy section of detailed laws of good human conduct from whose Hebrew opening words the portion of **Kedoshim** gets its traditional name: "Be holy, for I HaShem your God am Holy" (Leviticus 19:2).

These laws begin with the reverence one must show to one's parents, the observance of God's Sabbaths, the prohibition of making idols, leading into the rules that must govern every good society: support for the poor, the prohibition of theft, lying and dishonesty, of taking God's name in vain, business malpractice, injustice, slander, causeless hatred and other evil behaviors.

"Do not steal, do not deceive and do not lie to one another. Don't impound your friend's money, don't delay payment for services rendered. Don't unjustly favor either the poor or the rich. Don't hate your brother in your heart, give due reproof, do not take vengeance or nurse a grievance against the children of your people, and **love your neighbor as yourself**, for I am HaShem" (Leviticus 19:11-18).

Elsewhere the Torah teaches us to love God (Deuteronomy 6:5). In the injunction to "love your neighbor as yourself" we see that the love and service of God includes showing a love to one's fellow humans comparable to the love one has for oneself. For just as I am God's child, so are all my human brothers and sisters.

The word **love** is used in many different ways. Obviously the Torah cannot here be talking about romantically loving everyone else, if only for the reason that the love one has for oneself is not love in the romantic sense. Our love for ourselves is what generally makes us want what we think to be in our own interests while avoiding what may hurt or harm us. It is a comparable love that the Torah asks us to offer to our neighbors - those we live with in the home, in the neighborhood, at school, at work, in the community and in the wider world - to the maximum extent possible.

So fundamental is this rule that the great Torah sage Hillel said: "That which is hateful to you, do not do to your fellow. That is the whole Torah. The rest is the explanation: go and learn" (Talmud Shabbat 31a).

Some of the basic human loving practices towards neighbors included in this overall rule are listed by Rabbi Moses Maimonides in his Torah code (Laws of Mourning 16:1): "Visiting the sick; comforting mourners; respectful burial of the dead; giving practical assistance to couples who are getting married and celebrating with them, hospitality to travelers, practical acts of kindness to others. all the things that you would want others to do for you, you do for them."

This would surely include showing fundamental human politeness to all others wherever possible, including even to complete strangers and even when no specific "act of kindness" is called for.

The greatest love

Everyone wants good for themselves. The greatest good of all is God, who is all good and all love. Therefore, all who connect themselves to God through acts of service and devotion - each in his or her own way - are on the pathway to true and eternal good. If we can help others discover and pursue this good, we are showing them the truest love. At the same time, we are also loving ourselves! For through all our words and deeds spreading this love to our fellows, we ourselves gain greater connection with God.

Showing others the path is through trying under all circumstances to behave in the best possible manner in accordance with Torah teaching. One should also where possible practice introducing ideas, words and expressions of faith in God into one's various conversations with people at all kinds of junctures in life, endeavoring to speak in way that includes due expressions of thanks and praise to God and acknowledgement that He rules over everything.

One may thus become God's ambassador, each on his or her own level, shining the Torah to one's fellow humans through good deeds and kind words, without force or coercion, through the power of love and compassion, peace and truth.

World Class Events

Certain major sports events are reportedly watched live on TV every week by hundreds of millions of viewers across the world. A handful of performances by celebrity entertainers are said to have been watched by over a billion, while in 1997 the funeral of a British royal princess killed in a car crash is said to have commanded an audience of 2 billion people.

The fascination that royalty has for people all over the world may attest to a deep-seated yearning in humanity for a truly noble, pure, thoroughbred elite devoted to lives of special service for the benefit of the world.

Much of the book of Leviticus is devoted to the various Temple services and the Cohen priests who conducted them. Our present portion of **Emor** sets forth the exceptionally high standards of morality, personal and ritual purity and even physical appearance required of this "royal" elite of Cohen priests. The portion then goes on to detail their special Temple services on each of the great festivals of the annual cycle (Leviticus 23:1-44) - services conducted under the scrutiny of millions of pilgrims assembled in Jerusalem. With the rebuilding of the Temple in time to come, these services will also be seen to have the status of world class events, and will perhaps be viewed live by billions across the globe!

The festivals and the ecology

The three main festivals of the year - Pesach ("Passover"), Shavuot ("Feast of Weeks") and Succot ("Festival of Booths", "Tabernacles") - are celebrated by Jews wherever in the world they may be. But in Temple times the central focus of the festival observances is in Jerusalem in the main Temple courtyard, where each of the three festivals is to be marked in its own unique way as laid down in our portion.

The Rabbis taught that there are specified times during the year when the world is judged in the Heavenly Court (Mishnah Rosh Hashanah 1:2). The judgment on Pesach determines the success of our staple grain crops; the judgment on Shavuot determines the success of the fruits, while the judgment on Succot determines the rainfall, which is the key to the entire water ecology.

It is evident from the section of our portion dealing with the annual cycle of the festivals that the specific observances on each of the three pilgrim festivals relate intimately to the respective subject of the judgment on that festival. In the land of Israel, Pesach coincides with the beginning of the grain harvesting season, which was ceremonially inaugurated in the Temple with the Omer offering of barley - Israel's earliest-ripening grain species - on the second day of the festival (Lev. 23:9-14).

Fifty days later, at the height of the wheat-harvesting, Shavuot was celebrated with the presentation at the Temple Altar of two loaves of wheat bread, a ceremonial offering of the "first fruits" of the nation's agricultural endeavors (Lev. 23:17-21).

In Israel, Succot coincides with the end of the dry summer harvesting season, when people are starting to think of the need for rains for the success of next year's crops. On each of the days of the Succot festival, the Temple services included solemn processions around the Altar with branches and fruit from four species of trees that particularly exemplify our complete dependency upon God's merciful gift of water: the palm tree, myrtle bush, willow tree and citron (Lev. 23:39-41).

Economic health

Today's news media give the impression that the health of the economy depends on wise decisions by governments and financial leaders (rare indeed) together with such factors as consumer and investor optimism (severely damaged). At the same time the world reels from one ecological disaster to another, with widespread drought, chronic water shortage, crop failures, animal diseases and more.

The Torah is teaching us that ecological balance, harmony, blessing and prosperity depend upon God's mercy, which is all the more forthcoming when humanity humbly acknowledges and respects His great kindness in providing us with all our needs through the sunshine, rains, winds, vegetation, animals and birds and other creations that feed and sustain us.

The prophet teaches that after the cataclysms of the end of days, all the nations that survive will observe the Succot festival, which will then be a "world-class" annual event. It will be clear to everyone that the very rainfall depends upon this:

"And it shall come to pass that every one that is left of all the nations that came against Jerusalem shall go up from year to year to worship the King, HaShem of hosts, and to keep the feast of Tabernacles. And it shall be that if any of the families of the earth does not go up to Jerusalem to worship the King, HaShem of hosts, upon them there shall be no rain" (Zechariah 14:16-17).

The solemn observance of the festivals by the Cohen priests in the Temple in Jerusalem is of vital concern to all humanity since the world's sustainability and prosperity depend upon them.

Blasphemy

Those who scoff at this idea are in the category of the Blasphemer of God's Name as described in the episode at the end of our portion (Leviticus 10-23).

So serious is the prohibition of the willful, blatant cursing and disparagement of God's Name that it is the second of the Seven Noahide Commandments. The scoffer lives on God's earth, benefiting from all the gifts of His creation, yet arrogantly refuses to admit our fragile dependency on His tender mercies. Instead he shamelessly spews forth denigration and atheism in front of everyone, as has now become fashionable on the part of certain prominent secular philosophers turned media celebrities.

Let a single one of them see if he can have any influence on the rainfall when needed!

The Earth Belongs to God

The two portions of **Behar** and **Bechukotai** (which in many years are read on the same Sabbath), put the seal on the book of Leviticus, which together with the latter part of Exodus covers all the laws given to the people of Israel in the Covenant at Mount Sinai. The book of Numbers then tells the story of the people's journey through the wilderness to the Promised Land of Israel, while in Deuteronomy, as they stood poised to enter the Land, Moses reviewed all the laws of the Covenant.

The Earth belongs to God

The theme of the portion of **Behar** is property and ownership, particularly the ownership of land, which provides us not only with our living space but with all the food and other resources we consume.

Today well over half of humanity are crammed into great urban agglomerations, and the majority have little or no connection with the farmlands that produce their food. **Behar** invites us to consider a very different world of Israelite small farm-owners, who are at perfect liberty to plant, tend and harvest their crops for six years, but are commanded to cease all agricultural labor in the seventh "Sabbatical" year, forcing them to trust in God to bless their endeavors and provide their needs. To a person who may feel he can barely survive when he does till his land, it is no mean challenge to be told that for one year out of every seven he may not even do this!

The law of the Sabbatical year comes to teach the farmer that even if he sees himself as the "owner" of the land he farms, ultimately the land does not really belong to him but to the One who is the Owner of Everything. God gives the Israelite farmer license to work the land for six years, but revokes this license every seventh year to impress upon us that even with all the efforts we have to make to feed and sustain ourselves, we are always dependent on God to bless these efforts and provide us with our needs.

Humans have a natural tendency to believe that "it is *my* power and the strength of *my* hand that provides me with this prosperity" (Deuteronomy 8:17), and this belief is usually coupled with the urge to acquire ever more material wealth, as if this can give security. But the lesson of the Sabbatical year is that security comes not from human efforts alone but through God's blessing. For: "The earth and its fullness belong to God; the world, and those who dwell in it" (Psalms 24:1).

"Hear this, all you peoples; give ear, all you inhabitants of the world... rich and poor together. As to those who trust in their wealth, and boast themselves in the multitude of their riches: no man can by any means redeem his brother, nor give to God a ransom for him... Even wise men die, the foolish and brutish perish together, and leave their wealth to others. Their inward thought is that their houses shall continue forever and their dwelling-places to all generations; **they call their lands after their own names**. But man does not remain in honor; he is like the beasts that perish" (Psalms 49:2-3; 7-8; 11-13).

Humans "call their lands after their own names", but the Sabbatical year comes to remind us that we are not the real owners, and in the end the land reverts to its true Owner.

The laws of the Sabbatical and Jubilee years contained in **Behar** apply only to Israelites in the Land of Israel. They are not part of the Noahide code of Torah law, and gentiles are under no obligation to cease agricultural work on their own land in these years. However, just as the annual cycle of the festivals of Israel have significance not only for the people of Israel but for all the nations (as discussed in the Torah for the Nations commentary on **Emor**), so too Israel's observance of the Sabbatical cycles carries a message for all humanity.

The futile race for wealth

Most of the world today is caught up in a race for ever greater prosperity, and thus the worst possible "illness" is thought to be economic recession, when the gross domestic product of countries enters into decline, with the result that people literally become poorer. Yet the greater humanity's efforts to get wealthier, the more they seem to be frustrated by a succession of natural and other calamities that belie the assumption that "it is *my* power and the strength of *my* hand that provides me with this prosperity".

Approximately 40% of the world's agricultural land is now seriously degraded. Between 1950 and 1984, the so-called "Green Revolution" led to a 250% increase in world grain production, but much of this gain is non-sustainable, and there are signs that not only are new technologies reaching their peak of assistance, but they may now be contributing to soil contamination and the decline of arable land. Severe drought is plaguing countries in the Horn of Africa, the Middle East, Central Asia, Central America and Australia. With the steady exhaustion of food resources, over-drafting of groundwater, wars, internal struggles and economic failure, famine is a worldwide problem causing widespread destitution, malnutrition and heightened mortality. Leading experts on agricultural commodities foresee "mass starvation" in the event of a major North American crop failure.

One of the most startling signs that the earth itself is "rebelling" against humanity's unceasing and unthinking quest for ever greater prosperity is the mysterious collapse in the global population of the humble honeybees, which are required for the pollination of flowering plants and which pollinate 90% of commercial crops worldwide, including most fruits and vegetables, nuts, sunflowers, coffee, soy beans, cattle feed and even cotton. The last four years have seen the death of billions of honeybees world-wide, and scientists are no nearer to knowing what is causing the catastrophic fall in numbers.

The Blessings and the Curses

Most of the portion of **Bechukotai** is taken up with God's promises of the great blessings that ensue from following the commandments of the Torah and the terrible curses that result from ignoring and violating them.

"And if for all this you will not listen to Me but walk contrary to Me, then I will walk contrary unto you in fury; and I also will chastise you seven times for your sins" (Leviticus 26:27-8).

The Torah invites humanity to observe God's laws so as to enjoy the great benefits they bring. If we refuse, we lay ourselves open to the dangers of God's chastisements, which fly in the face of our human illusions of grandeur and power, coming to prove that despite what we may think, "The earth and its fullness belong to God".

The Beauty of Diversity

The book of Numbers - fourth of the Five Books of Moses - opens with the people of Israel still encamped at the foot of Mount Sinai after receiving the Torah, but now poised to leave on their journey to their promised homeland where their mission would be to practice what they had been taught. For: "The main thing is not study but practical action" (Ethics of the Fathers 1:17).

Prior to the people's departure from Sinai, Moses was instructed to take a census of the Twelve Tribes and assign them to their positions both when encamped and when marching, and to assign to the various families of the Levites their respective duties relating to the Sanctuary, which was to be the central focus of the nation's life.

The figures of Moses' count recorded in our portion give the book of Numbers its traditional English name. For many Bible students the significance of the many details contained in this "national archive" of the people of Israel may be obscure. Yet it is noteworthy that the positions of the various tribes and families around the Sanctuary were by no means random.

"And God spoke to Moses and to Aaron, saying: 'The children of Israel shall encamp each man by his flag according to the emblems of their paternal houses; they shall encamp at a distance facing the Tent of Meeting'" (Numbers 2:1-2).

Each of the tribes had their own ensign relating to the unique attributes of that tribe. For example, the sign of Judah, the royal tribe, was the lion, king of the beasts; that of Zebulun, a tribe of merchants, was a ship, while that of Issachar, famed for their astronomical knowledge, was the sun and the moon. The assigned positions of each tribe in groups to the east, south, north or west of the sanctuary were also bound up with their distinctive character traits, for in Torah teaching the directions of the compass all have their own special connotations. East, where the sun rises, signifies blessing, west signifies receiving, while south and north respectively signify kindness and strength.

The Torah here teaches us that we are not all required to try to be the same as one another, because each one of us is God's unique creation, each with his or her own distinctive gifts and attributes.

"The greatness of the King of the kings of kings, the Holy One blessed be He, is seen in the fact that while a man may make many coins with one mould, all identical with one another, the Holy One blessed be He stamps every human in the mould of the archetypal Adam, yet not a single one is identical with any other" (Sanhedrin 38a).

What we must do is to learn how to dwell with one another together in harmony despite the many differences between us all. This can be done when everyone knows that they have their own special place, mission and function as part of God's greater purpose, signified by the Sanctuary itself, which everyone had to face from a respectful distance.

Throughout history, diversity has been and continues until this very day to be a source of conflict within and between families, social groups, nations and races, each attempting to dominate others and coerce them to their will and viewpoint. Too often people find it easier to continue old patterns of aggression and warfare instead of striving to make peace, which can only be done when we accept that within the transcendent unity of God there is room for different outlooks, viewpoints and ways of life, and that they can coexist peaceably as long as we agree on certain common denominators - above all, the prohibition of violence and murder, robbery and injustice, which are among the main pillars of the Universal Noahide Code of Law. If we will all look towards God's "Sanctuary" - the Noahide Code, which contains the blueprint for universal peace - we will be able to live side by side with each other, all fulfilling their own unique mission in God's greater plan.

Israel does not call upon all the peoples of the world to give up their own identity, individuality and traditions in order to convert to Judaism. Rather, they invite all nations to pursue their own unique missions and interests within the boundaries of what is permitted under the Noahide Code, while eschewing aggression, wanton violence and killing, exploitation and other prohibited behaviors.

Through increasing knowledge and awareness of God - Who transcends all opposites and contradictions - it will eventually be possible for all the different types and kinds of people to coexist peacefully, as in Isaiah's prophetic allegory:

"And the wolf shall dwell with the lamb, and the leopard shall lie down with the kid; and the calf and the young lion and the fatling together; and a little child shall lead them. They shall not hurt nor destroy in all My holy mountain; for the earth shall be full of the knowledge of HaShem, as the waters cover the sea" (Isaiah 11:6).

Owning Up

A cherished part of American folklore is the story of how as a boy, George Washington, later to become first president of the United States, chopped down his father's cherry tree and, when asked about it, bravely and honestly admitted his deed in the famous words: "Father I cannot tell a lie, I did it with my little hatchet." To which his father replied: "My son, that you should not be afraid to tell the truth is worth more to me than a thousand trees."

Regardless of whether it actually happened as told, the story illustrates the beauty of admitting the truth even if it shows us to be less virtuous than we would have others believe.

After impulsively or purposely carrying out a wrongful act for the sake of some pleasure or other imagined advantage, it is a deep-seated human instinct to evade responsibility, as when Cain, the first murderer, pretended not to know the whereabouts of his slain brother (Genesis 4:9). It takes courage to "own up" - to admit oneself to be the "owner" and perpetrator of the wrong - submitting oneself to the necessary consequences in order to make restitution.

Evasion

For a child, the price of admitting having cut down a tree may be little more than a telling-off and spanking. But the older, better-known and more respectable people become, the harder it may be for them to own up to their mistakes. Civilized society depends upon integrity and trust, and when a person has a public persona of rectitude, their own pride, the fear of shame and other pressures may make the price of truthfulness seem too high to pay. We are not angels: people commit all kinds of wrongs, small and great, and the usual tendency is either to seek to justify them or to take flight into denial, fibs, lies and cover-ups.

This is particularly visible in public life today, where many different leaders and other influential figures, whether in national and international politics, big business, industry, banking, medicine, science and other spheres, have been responsible for all kinds of misdeeds, wrong decisions and policies that have led to disastrous consequences, often through a negligence that can only be described as criminal. [A few random examples currently in the news might include the enormous scandals surrounding the recent economic "meltdown" and bank failures that have greatly enriched certain players; corporate and government handling of the British Petroleum oil-spill; evidence of academic rigging of global-warming statistics; unresolved questions surrounding 9/11, the claims used to justify the launching of the Iraqi war, the global flu "epidemics"; the marketing of faulty automobiles, and many more.]

The most "advanced" countries in the world have never had more surveillance cameras monitoring not only motorist breaches of traffic regulations but every other kind of behavior on the streets, in all public places, shops, banks, restaurants, hotels, stations, airports etc. Concurrently, the unending stream of revelations about public scams in politics, government, police, banking, business and other spheres indicate no less a level of sophistication in the use of Enron-style paper-shredders and other methods of destroying, hiding or disguising any evidence and tell-tale tracks that might reveal the full extent of the wrongdoing and corruption practiced today at the highest levels.

Rare indeed today is the leader that has the courage to stand up and publicly admit to his errors and misdeeds.

The Torah ethic

Contrast the ethic taught by the Torah in our present portion:

"And God said to Moses: 'Tell the children of Israel: If a man or a woman commit any sin that men commit, perpetrating a trespass against God, that soul shall be guilty. Then they must **confess** their sin that they carried out; and they must make restitution in full for their guilt... and give it to the person they wronged" (Numbers 5:6-7).

The Torah sages teach us that this verse comes to supplement the verse in Leviticus 5:21: "When a soul sins and perpetrates a trespass against God, dealing falsely with his neighbor in the matter of a deposit or pledge or robbery or oppression."

The sages commented:

"Why is dealing falsely with one's neighbor called a 'trespass against God'? Because anyone who gives a loan or does business with another does so in the presence of witnesses and with a written contract, so that if the other party comes to lie about it, he is lying in the face of the witnesses or the contract. But when a person deposits valuables with another for safekeeping, he does not want any other soul to know about it except the 'third party between them' (i.e. God, who is all-seeing). Therefore if the trustee later denies ever having received the deposit, he is lying against the 'third party between them'" (Rashi on Leviticus 5:21).

This explains why seeking to deny or cover-up a crime or misdeed against another person is also a denial of God, and for this reason the previously-quoted verse in our portion (Numbers 5:7) teaches that it is insufficient for the perpetrator merely to make financial restitution to the victim of his wrongdoing. He must also formally confess his wrongdoing before God and undertake never to repeat it.

Thus we see that there are three steps in making amends for wrongdoing:

1. Correcting the wrong (where possible) by making full financial restitution to the victim of the wrongdoing.

2. Appeasing the victim.

3. Confessing to God.

Confession

In the words of Rabbi Moses Maimonides ("Rambam", c. 1137-1204) in his comprehensive Torah law code, the Mishneh Torah, Laws of Repentance:

"If a person transgresses any law of the Torah, whether a positive commandment or a prohibition, whether with brazen intention or unwittingly, when he wants to repent and turn aside from his sin, he is obliged to make confession before God, blessed be He, as it is written: 'If a man or a woman commit any sin... they must confess their sin that they carried out' (Numbers 5:6-7). This means making verbal confession.

How does one confess? One says, "Please, O God, I have sinned, transgressed and rebelled before You and I did such and such, and I regret it and I am ashamed of my deeds and I will never return to this.'

Likewise those liable to sin and guilt offerings would not secure atonement through their sacrifices until they repented and made verbal confession. Likewise, if one has injured his fellow or caused damage to his property, even if he pays him what he owes him, he does not secure atonement until he confesses and turns from ever doing anything similar" (Laws of Repentance 1:1).

It takes great courage to follow this pathway, but only through the necessary truth, honesty and tears of shame and contrition can one come to the joy of being clean with God and man.

It is far better to confess our wrongdoings while still alive in this world than to seek refuge in denial and cover-ups. For God is present everywhere and requires no surveillance cameras or other devices to record our every deed, word and thought. In the words of the Torah sages: "Focus on three things and you will not come to sin. Know what is above you: a seeing eye, a listening ear, and all your actions written in a book" (Ethics of the Fathers 2:1). When the time comes for each person's judgment after death, the book is opened and the recording is replayed. With no possibility of flight or denial, they must admit responsibility for all their deeds and suffer the consequences.

David, King of Israel, exemplar of the true leader, never claimed to be perfect. When he sinned, he admitted it, teaching all humanity the path of repentance:

"Be gracious to me, O God, according to Your mercy; according to the multitude of Your compassions erase my transgressions. Wash me thoroughly from my iniquity and cleanse me from my sin. For I know my transgressions; and my sin is ever before me... Behold, You desire truth in the inward parts; let me therefore know wisdom in my inmost heart. Make me hear joy and gladness, that the bones which You have crushed may rejoice. Hide Your face from my sins, and blot out all my iniquities. Create in me a pure heart, O G-d; and renew a steadfast spirit within me. Do not cast me away from Your presence; and do not take Your holy spirit from me. Restore to me the joy of Your salvation and let a willing spirit uphold me. Then will I teach transgressors Your ways, and sinners shall return unto You... O Lord, open my lips and my mouth shall declare Your praise. For you do not delight in sacrifice, or else would I give it; You have no pleasure in a burnt-offering. The sacrifices of God are a broken spirit; a broken and a contrite heart, O God, You will not despise." (Psalms 51:3-5, 8-15, 17-19).

Unity within Diversity

"And God spoke to Moses, saying: 'Speak to Aaron and say to him: When you light the lamps, the seven lamps shall give light in front of the candlestick. And this was the work of the candlestick, beaten work of gold. according to the pattern which God had shown Moses, so he made the candlestick."

Numbers 8:2, 4

Continuing on from the last two portions explaining the arrangements in the Sanctuary, our present portion opens with instructions to the High Priest about the daily kindling of the lights of the Candelabrum (Menorah). In parallel, this week's prophetic passage ("Haftara") traditionally read after the weekly Synagogue Torah reading includes Zechariah's vision of the heavenly candelabrum (Zechariah 4:2-3).

The design of the Temple candelabrum, with its central shaft and six branches, each supporting one of its seven lamps and adorned with decorative cups, knops and flowers, is set forth in Exodus 25:31-37. All of these components were to be made specifically **"of one piece: the whole of it one beaten work of pure gold"**(verse 36).

This comes to teach us that diverse elements (the seven branches and their ornaments) can co-exist in unity (one piece of gold).

Sevens in Nature

The natural creation was traditionally thought to be made up of sevens, such as the seven continents, seven seas and seven classical planets (the Sun, Moon, Mercury, Venus, Mars, Jupiter, and Saturn). From the names of these planets come the names of the seven days of our week.

The theme of seven recurs throughout the Torah, the opening verse of which contains seven Hebrew words introducing the account of Creation in seven "days" (Genesis 1).

The sign of God's Covenant with humanity after Noah's flood was the rainbow (Genesis 9:13-16). This consists of the seven chief colors: red, orange, yellow, green, blue, indigo and violet. All are refractions of white light: the different hues lie adjacent to and work with one another, so that the rainbow shines as one whole through the coherence and harmony of its component parts.

Unity amidst diversity

The seven-branched Temple Candelabrum, the Menorah, is a universal symbol of unity amidst diversity. Significantly, Torah law forbids one to make a candelabrum for one's own personal use in the same form as that of the Temple Menorah

(Maimonides, Mishneh Torah, Laws of the Temple 7:10). The Menorah cannot be someone's private, personal property. There can only be one Menorah: that of the Temple, dedicated to the glory of God and not to the glorification of any specific individual or group. (The Chanukah candelabrum lit annually in private homes and many public locations has *eight* branches, relating to the eight days of the Chanukah festival commemorating the Second Temple miracle when one remaining flask of pure oil was sufficient to kindle the Menorah for eight days.)

The Temple was in no need of a lamp to provide interior lighting, because the Temple itself emanates light! The daily kindling of the Menorah by the priest was intended to radiate the light of God and His Torah from the Temple out to the entire world.

Just as the seven colors of the rainbow emanate from one source of white light, so the seven branches of the Menorah make up a single "tree" of light. Its seven branches allude to the seven chief attributes from which the astonishing plurality and diversity of the world around us derives: Kindness, Strength, Harmony, Victory, Splendor, Purity and Kingship.

Correspondingly, the human face has its own seven "lights": two eyes, two ears, two nostrils and one mouth, which rules over us like a king.

In the words of Rabbi Nachman of Breslov:

To gain spiritual understanding and awareness, you must sanctify the seven "lamps" of your head: your mouth, nostrils, ears and eyes. Guard your **mouth** from speaking any falsehood; through humility and patience, sanctify your **nostrils** with the fear of Heaven, as it is written: "...he will *scent* the fear of God" (Isaiah 11:3). Use your **ears** to attend to the words of the wise: believe in what they say. Lower your **eyes** and avert them from evil. Sanctifying the seven "lamps" of the head can bring you to deeper spiritual understanding and awareness, and your heart will then burn with passion for God. These heights of understanding are a blessing from God that is bestowed from above without preliminaries and introductions: this is the gift of holy spirit.

Likutey Moharan I, 21

The seven branches of the Menorah also correspond to the Seven Universal Laws of the Children of Noah, with whom God struck His Covenant after the flood with the sign of the seven-colored rainbow.

A universal symbol

The universal relevance of the Menorah as a symbol of unity amidst diversity for all humanity finds expression in Psalm 67, a paean of thanksgiving to God by all the nations and a prayer for universal blessing:

For the Leader; with string-music; A Psalm, a Song:

1. God be gracious to us, and bless us; may He shine His face toward us; Selah!

2. That Your way may be known upon earth, Your salvation among all nations.

3. Let the peoples give thanks to You, O God; let the peoples give thanks to You, all of them.

4. Let the nations be glad and sing for joy; for You will judge the peoples with equity, and lead the nations upon earth. Selah

5. Let the peoples give thanks to You, O God; let the peoples give thanks to You, all of them.

6. The earth has yielded her increase; may God - our God - bless us.

7. May God bless us, and let all the ends of the earth fear Him.

Besides the first line, which is a title or superscription, this truly universal Psalm consists of seven verses. As an aid to prayer and meditation, the Hebrew text of this Psalm is often written in the form of the Menorah. Note that verse 4 is the longest of all: this forms the central shaft of the Menorah and its base, while verses 1-3 and 5-7 are arranged on either side, corresponding to the six branches.

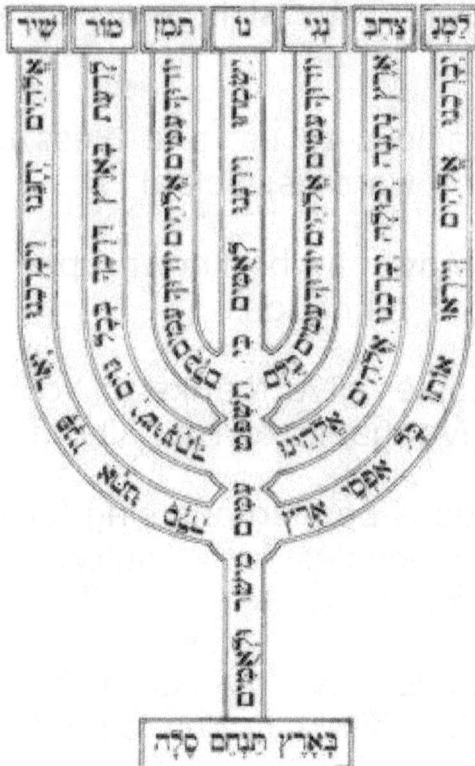

Psalm 67 written in Hebrew in form of Menorah.
Verse 1 is on left hand side, verse 7 on right hand side.

Seventy branches

When King Solomon built his Temple, he made ten golden candelabra which stood in two rows in front of the Menorah of Moses (II Chronicles 4:7, Talmud Tractate Shekalim 18a). These ten candelabra, each with its own seven branches, together had a total of seventy branches - corresponding to the seventy nations that developed from the offspring of Noah and his sons. All these individual branches, each with their own attributes and characteristics, derive their power from the refractions of the "colors" or "attributes" contained in the light emanating from seven branches of the archetypal Menorah of Moses, all made of one piece, corresponding to the colors of the rainbow, which are all refractions of unitary white light.

When all work together in harmony, there is peace!

Don't Just Follow the Crowd

The Torah does not hold back from exposing the failures and shortcomings of even the foremost leaders of Israel, in order to provide clear, true instruction for all the generations. A case in point is the story in our portion about the gratuitous slander spread by ten of the twelve tribal leaders whom Moses sent from the wilderness in order to tour and report on the Promised Land. Their slander brought a decree of death upon the entire generation of adults who accepted it, forty years of wandering in the wilderness for their children, the destruction of the First and Second Temples and numerous other tragedies in later generations.

It is surmised that the ten spies who brought back an evil report feared that as soon as the people would enter the Promised Land, they themselves would lose the prestigious positions of tribal leadership that they enjoyed in the wilderness. Accordingly they sought to paint a fearsome picture of a land inhabited by unconquerable giants and other enemies in order to strike terror into the hearts of the people and undermine their will to go there. Whether the spies really believed what they said or not, they presented a seemingly irrefutable case for abandoning the national mission because of apparently insurmountable obstacles.

The power of evil speech

The ten evil spies knew better than to spread outright lies about the Promised Land. They opened their report to Moses and the people by stating what everyone already knew - that it was indeed a land "flowing with milk and honey" (Numbers 13:21; cf. Exodus 3:8). For they well understood that "every falsehood that does not start with a modicum of truth will not stand up in the end" (Rashi ad loc.). Their success as slanderers lay in the skill with which they used "spin" to present a series of apparently undeniable "facts" that would automatically lead their listeners to draw exactly the conclusions they wanted them to draw:

"The land through which we passed to spy it out is a land that eats up its inhabitants, and all the people that we saw in it are men of great stature. There we saw the Nephilim, the sons of Anak (the giant). and we were in our own sight like grasshoppers, and so we were in their sight" (Numbers 13:32-33).

This last statement was the "punch line" that broke the people's hearts despite the intrinsic fallacy in their argument - because even if the spies *felt* like grasshoppers compared to the giants they saw, it did not necessarily follow that this was how those giants perceived them. Even a tiny creature like a wasp or a scorpion can strike terror in the heart of a much larger creature! But because the wicked spies had lost their confidence that God was with them, they lost their confidence in themselves!

The majority are not necessarily right

Yet two of the twelve spies refused to join in the conspiracy of the other ten. One was Joshua - leader of the tribe of Ephraim - who had from his youth been Moses' attendant (Numbers 11:28) and moreover received a special blessing from his master (ibid. 13:16). This was what gave Joshua the strength to resist the machinations of his fellow spies. But what was it that fortified Caleb, representative of the tribe of Judah, giving him the courage to stand up against ten tribal princes who undoubtedly wielded tremendous authority and influence?

Caleb evidently understood that the mere fact that the other ten spies were in the majority did not make them right.

The Torah itself teaches the principle that when leaders and judges do not concur in matters of national counsel and legal judgment, we are obliged to follow the majority view. However, this applies only when the majority opinion accords with Torah law, but not when the majority are bent on evil: "You shall not follow a multitude to do evil, neither shall you bear witness in a cause to turn aside after a multitude to pervert justice" (Exodus 23:2; see Rashi ad loc.).

Caleb courageously demonstrated his determination to abide by what was right and true even when he was in danger of being stoned by the mob.

And Caleb stilled the people toward Moses, and said: 'We should go up at once and possess it; for we are well able to overcome it' (Numbers 13:30).

'If God favors us, He will bring us into this land, and give it to us - a land flowing with milk and honey. Only do not rebel against God, and do not fear the people of the land... for God is with us; do not fear them' (ibid. 14:8-9).

Caleb and the "giants"

Caleb had seen the physically imposing giants that dwelled in the land, but he was not unnerved because he bound himself to far greater giants - giants of the spirit. These were the founding fathers of Israel, Abraham, Isaac and Jacob, to whom God had explicitly promised the land and who now lay in their resting place in the Cave of Machpelah in Hebron.

The Torah sages teach that while the other spies were proceeding with their tour of the land, Caleb - who already sensed their evil intentions - took a detour to visit Hebron to pray at the graves of the patriarchs. There is a hint of this in our portion in Numbers 13:22, where the text states that "*they* went up by the south and *he* came to Hebron". In the Hebrew text "*they* went" is a plural verb while "*he* came" is in the singular. That it was Caleb who stepped foot in Hebron is explicitly confirmed by the Biblical texts in Deuteronomy 1:36, Joshua ch. 14 vv. 9, 12 & 13 and ch. 15 vv. 13-14 and Judges 1:20.

It was not some baseless, overblown self-confidence that made Caleb imagine that the people of Israel could overcome the many obstacles that appeared to stand in their way in entering the Promised Land. Rather it was his absolute faith and trust in God's supreme power, which he fortified by binding himself to the patriarchs, the founding fathers of this faith. This was what gave Caleb the courage to defy the seeming giants that dwelled in Hebron, and to defy the authority and influence of ten leading "giants" and princes of his own people when he clearly saw that they were wrong.

Today's fearsome giants

Today many new breeds of "giants" stand in the way of those who seek to understand the true meaning and purpose of our lives in this world and who yearn to follow the Torah path of justice, goodness and kindness. Among these obstructing "giants" are the great media empires that hold millions and millions under the spell of their daily torrents of subtle, skillfully-crafted messages propagating the rejection of traditional faith and belief and the embrace of every kind of licentiousness. Other such giants are the tyrannical regimes, international organizations and other mass pressure groups that endlessly repeat blatant lies, shamelessly distorting the language of morality and ethics to rationalize cruel injustices.

From Caleb we must learn to have the courage not to go after the masses just because they may be a numerical majority, for this does not make them right. We must think for ourselves and fearlessly search for the truth, binding ourselves to the Torah - eternal fountain of truth - and to the righteous sages who have followed and taught it in all the generations.

For Heaven's Sake,
or Each For Himself?

"Every dispute that is for the sake of heaven will endure in the end, but one that is not for the sake of heaven will not endure in the end. Which dispute was for the sake of heaven? The dispute between Hillel and Shammai. And which was not for the sake of heaven? This is the dispute aroused by Korach and his assembly" (Ethics of the Fathers 5:17).

The Torah sages distinguish between two different kinds of disputes. The first is where the participants debate, argue and counter-argue "for the sake of heaven", seeking to clarify the true meaning and intent of God's Torah. As the classic example of this kind of dispute, the sages cite the wide-ranging legal discussions between the Torah academies of Hillel and Shamai, two leading scholars who lived around two thousand years ago, towards the end of the Second Temple period.

The other kind of dispute is where the real, underlying intent of at least one of the parties is not "for the sake of heaven" but for his own self-aggrandizement. The classic example of this kind of dispute is Korach's rebellion against the authority of Moses as described in our present portion.

Korach was a leading member of the tribe of Levites, whom Moses on God's instructions had appointed as the Temple guards and singers, as described in Numbers chapter 4. Yet despite this great honor, Korach was disgruntled when he saw that Moses - a member of the same tribe - was not only functioning as king over all the people but had also appointed his own brother Aaron with his sons to serve in the seemingly more prestigious role of Temple priests.

Korach wanted the kudos for himself, and in order to gain it he sought to turn the entire people against Moses and Aaron. He realized that the people had little to gain from merely exchanging one set of leaders for another, so in order to stir them up, he presented himself as a populist fighting for equal rights for all. Together with a powerful group of ambitious leaders who were similarly disgruntled, Korach rose up against Moses:

"And they assembled against Moses and against Aaron and said to them: 'You have taken too much upon yourselves, for all of the congregation are holy, every one of them, and God is among them. So why do you raise yourselves above the assembly of God?" (Numbers 16:3).

When the Torah sages define Korach's dispute against Moses as one that was not "for the sake of heaven", they are pointing out that he was not a disinterested party whose only concern was for truth to win out. Rather, he was motivated by his own pride. Unfortunately in the world in which we live this is true of very many of the disputes and divisions among different groups and factions, whether in politics or in other spheres. Even in coalitions of like-minded people, it often turns out that each is ultimately out for himself and his own interests. Few are the statesmen, thinkers and visionaries who have the ability to rise above egocentricity and work truly for the collective good.

However, this does not mean that we should cynically conclude that without exception, all disagreements and disputes between people of different viewpoints and opinions are doomed to be intrinsically vitiated by self-interest on the part of all those involved. It is possible to disagree with one another yet still conduct healthy debates and discussions about our differences with a view to clarifying the meaning and implications of the various viewpoints and opinions. The Torah sages endorsed the value of such debates when they cited the disputes between the academies of Hillel and Shammai as being "for the sake of heaven".

Hillel's 120-year lifetime is traditionally dated from 110 B.C.E. to 10 C.E. Hillel was the president of the Sanhedrin, the supreme council of Torah sages, while Shammai was his deputy (Avot 1:12). The two had very different characters. Hillel was a model of meekness, patience and loving kindness, while Shammai, a building surveyor by profession, was strict, rigorous and punctilious. Their differing approaches complemented one another.

Until their time, there had been very few disputes among the mainstream rabbis over the interpretation of the Bible text and the practical directives that were to be derived from it. However, the respective students of Hillel and Shammai became two schools espousing radically different approaches. They shared a fundamental acceptance of the Bible text and its laws - the "Written Torah" - together with all the main tenets of the Oral Law. Where they differed was in the ways in which they derived practical directives from the received tradition. Yet despite their disagreements, the later sages emphasized that members of the two rival academies loved one another, and far from turning into two warring factions, they even intermarried with one another (Mishnah Yevamot 1:4). They were able to love one another because they shared a common love for the Torah.

The consensus of the later Torah sages is that in practice the law in almost all cases follows the opinion of the Academy of Hillel, but this does not mean that the Academy of Shammai were in some sense "wrong". Indeed the teachings of the latter are studied by Torah scholars until today just as much as those of the Academy of Hillel, because they help us to deepen our understanding of God's Torah. For the Torah - the repository of God's infinite wisdom - is like an edifice so vast and magnificent that no one person can grasp it all in its totality. From different vantage points different facets are visible. Just as each individual sees what he sees from his own vantage point, so he can benefit from striving to understand what others see from *their* vantage points.

Rabbi Abba said in the name of Shmuel: For three years the Academy of Shammai and the Academy of Hillel argued with one another, each saying that the practical legal directives were in accordance with their own viewpoints, until a heavenly voice declared that "these and these are the words of the Living God but the legal decisions are in accordance with the positions of the Academy of Hillel". Now if "these and these are the words of the Living God", what made the Academy of Hillel worthy of having the law decided in accordance with their viewpoint? It was because they were easy-going and long-suffering, and they studied not only their own teachings but also those of the Academy of Shammai. Moreover, they even gave precedence to the teachings of the Academy of Shammai over their own teachings! (Babylonian Talmud, Eiruvin 13b).

The debates of the followers of Hillel and Shammai are a model for civilized enquiry and discussion, where the purpose of the participants is more than just to refute and humiliate one another, but to clarify and elucidate the truth.

God has created a world of amazing diversity and variety. We pray and hope for the day when those with different viewpoints and opinions will be able to coexist in peace and harmony.

"And the wolf shall dwell with the lamb, and the leopard shall lie down with the kid; and the calf and the young lion and the fatling together; and a little child shall lead them. And the cow and the bear will feed; their young ones shall lie down together; and the lion shall eat straw like the ox. And the suckling child shall play on the hole of the viper, and the weaned child shall put his hand on the serpent's den. They shall not hurt nor destroy in all My holy mountain; for the earth shall be full of the knowledge of God as the waters cover the sea." (Isaiah 11:6-9).

Inner Purity

"This is the statute of the law which God has commanded, saying: Speak to the children of Israel, that they bring you a red heifer that is faultless with no blemish on it and on which no yoke ever came" (Numbers 19:2).

The opening chapter of our portion teaches how the Cohen-priests of Israel are to prepare the ashes of the Red Heifer to be used in the ritual purification of those who have been defiled through physically touching or even being in the same building as a human corpse, dead bones, other body parts or a grave.

Our text teaches that the priest is to take a perfectly red heifer that has never been made to work. Facing the Temple, he slaughters it on a woodpile and burns it to ashes. The ashes are cast into a flask of pure spring water and drops of the mixture are sprinkled with a sprig of hyssop upon those who have become defiled through contact with a dead body etc. They must undergo a seven-day cycle of purification, being sprinkled on the third and seventh days. The final step of the cycle is to immerse their entire head and body in a ritual pool of natural waters. Only then are they permitted to enter the Temple courtyard and partake of holy sacrificial portions or tithes.

This commandment is of particular relevance to the Cohen priests, since it is their function to serve in the Temple and much of their food consists of tithes. The priests are explicitly commanded to avoid all defilement from contact with dead bodies except in the case of the burial of close family members (Leviticus 21:1ff).

On the other hand, the laws of defilement from contact with the dead impinge little on the everyday lives of most ordinary Israelites even after some kind of contact with a dead body etc. Only if they want to enter the Temple precincts must they first undergo the necessary purification.

In our time it is impossible to practice this commandment as nobody has yet found a perfectly red heifer meeting all the necessary requirements. Nevertheless, efforts are afoot to locate or breed a suitable animal and to reinstate fulfillment of this commandment as part of the process of building the Third Temple in Jerusalem.

What does it mean?

The Torah introduces the commandment of the Red Heifer with the words: "This is the **statute** of the Torah which God commanded." It is said that even King Solomon - who understood the reasons for all the commandments - could not fathom the true meaning and purpose of the Red Heifer. This is what he meant when he wrote: "I said I would get wisdom, but it was far from me" (Ecclesiastes 7:23; Midrash Rabba 19:3).

In the words of Rashi, prince of the rabbinical Bible commentators (**Ra**bbi **Sh**lomo **I**tzhaki 1040-1105): "Because the Satan and the peoples of the world taunt Israel, asking, 'What is this commandment and what is its rationale?' the word **statute** is written, indicating that this is a **decree** of God, and you are not at liberty to raise doubts about it" (Rashi on Numbers 19:2).

The idea that contact with a human corpse or body part somehow "defiles" a person is no less mysterious than the purification process through the ashes of the Red Heifer. Corpses or body parts are things almost all people understandably prefer to keep well away from, and may engender great sorrow and even disgust. But while these feelings may be palpable, the ritual "defilement" itself is quite invisible, has no substance and could not be detected in the defiled person by any physical instrument.

Defilement through contact with a dead body, body parts or graves is but one of a number of radically different types of ritual defilement (Hebrew: *tum'ah*) found in the Torah text that affect not only the person who had direct contact but in some cases other people and even chairs, beds, garments, utensils, food and drink that they touch. The different kinds of defilement arise from:

- Carrying or having physical contact with even small parts of animal and bird cadavers (Leviticus 11:24-35)
- Emission of seed and sexual intercourse (Leviticus 15:16-18; Deuteronomy 23:11)
- A menstruating woman (Leviticus 15:19)
- A mother after childbirth (Leviticus 12:4-5)
- Morbid flows of non-menstrual blood in women and gonorrheal-type emissions from the male ember (Leviticus 15:1-15; ibid. vv. 25-30)
- Contact with Biblical leprosy (*Tzara'at*) manifested by morbid patches on the skin of the body and head, on certain garments and the walls of houses (Leviticus ch 13ff)

It is obvious that the various categories of "defilement" are all quite different from one another. For example, although the Torah decrees that sexual intercourse and menstruation give rise to their own associated unique kinds of "defilement", these are perfectly natural human functions, and can in no way be compared with biblical leprosy, which is clearly a morbid condition.

The waters of purification

Each of the different kinds of defilement has its own unique process of purification. The one thing that all the different kinds of purification processes have in common that they all require immersion in a ritual pool of natural waters.

In the words of the outstanding codifier of Torah law, Rabbi Moses Maimonides (1135-1204):

It is clear and evident that the various different kinds of defilement and their methods of purification are decrees laid down by the written law and are not susceptible to human reason: they are inscrutable Torah statutes. The same applies to immersion in water in order to be purified from the various different kinds of defilement. For defilement - *tum'ah* - is not like physical mud or filth that can be washed off with water. Ritual purification through immersion is a decree of the written law, and **its efficacy depends on the person's inner intention**. The sages therefore stated that if a person immerses without the proper intention, it is just as if he has not immersed at all.

Although this is ultimately beyond our ability to understand, it does contain an important allusion. We see that when a person has the heartfelt intention of purifying himself, just as soon as he immerses in the water he is ritually pure even though nothing has changed in his physical body.

Likewise when a person steers his heart to purify his soul from the various kinds of spiritual impurities - wicked thoughts, evil traits and attitudes - just as soon as he fully commits himself to cease following his evil promptings, immersing his soul in the waters of Godly knowledge and understanding, he is pure.

Thus it says: 'I have sprinkled upon you pure waters, and you shall be purified from all your impurities, and from all your abominations I shall purify you' (Ezekiel 36:25). Likewise, God in His abundant mercies purifies the person from all sin, transgression and guilt. Amen.

(Maimonides, Mishneh Torah, Laws of Ritual Pools 11:12)

The fact that ritual defilement may be physically undetectable does not mean it has no reality. Similarly, people's thoughts and instincts may be physically undetectable but they have a decisive effect upon their lives and conduct.

The things that really have the power to "defile" our lives and behavior are negative traits and attitudes such as causeless hatred, jealousy, vengefulness, cruelty, excessive physical lust and the like. These are the maladies of the soul. To purify ourselves from them may take a lengthy process of purification. A crucial part of the process is to immerse ourselves in the waters of the Torah of the Living God with the inner intention of purifying and improving ourselves through the implementation of its teachings in our actual practical lives.

The Evil Eye

Our portion is named after Balak, king of Moab, who sought to put a curse upon the Children of Israel in the hope of frustrating their forward march to the Promised Land. Yet the central character in this portion's extraordinary narrative is undoubtedly Bilaam - considered as the greatest of all the gentile prophets - whose services King Balak solicited in order to mouth the curse.

Arrogance, lust and the evil eye

The Torah sages (Avot 5:19) characterized Bilaam and all who follow in his path as having three distinctive traits: an **arrogant spirit, un-restrained lust** and an **evil eye**.

*Rashi on Numbers chapter 22 vv. 13 & 18 and chapter 24 v. 2 explains how the Biblical texts support this characterization. Numbers 22:13: "Bilaam rose up in the morning, and said to the princes of Balak: 'Go back to your land, for God refuses to give me leave to go with **you** ' " - Bilaam was demanding higher level emissaries commensurate with his supposed dignity. Numbers 22:18: " And Bilaam answered and said to the servants of Balak: 'If Balak would give me his house **full of silver and gold**, I cannot go beyond* *the word of God.' - i.e. Bilaam desired enormous wealth. Numbers 24:2: "And Bilaam lifted up his **eyes** and he saw Israel dwelling tribe by tribe..." - he sought to put his evil eye upon them.*

It may be easy to understand how arrogance makes a person look upon the entire world as if it exists only to serve and aggrandize himself, while lust makes a person want to enjoy all the pleasures of the world to the full. (The Hebrew root of the name of Bilaam has the connotation of "devour", "consume".) But what exactly is the "evil eye"?

We might have thought that the human eye merely takes in an objective photograph of whatever stands before it. But the Torah teaches that people tend to see what they *want* to see. "Do not go about after your own **heart** and your own **eyes**, after which you are used to going astray" (Numbers 15:39). From this verse we learn that the promptings of a person's heart and their own self-interest tend to govern how they look out upon the world and interpret what they see, unless they take themselves in hand so as to achieve a more objective view and not to err in their vision. The eye is simply the instrument with which the mind sees. The "evil eye" is the vision of a person who allows the untrammeled selfishness, jealousy and vindictiveness in his own heart to determine what he "sees" when he looks out at the world around him.

The selfish, arrogant, lustful person tends mostly to see only deficiency all around, critically examining everyone else to find only their faults and inadequacies. Instead of marveling at the unending diversity, beauty and wonder of God's creation - the "overflowing goblet" - such a person sees only how "the cup is half-empty".

This is the very opposite of the generous spirit that God wants us to cultivate in commanding us "to go in all His ways" (Deuteronomy 11:22). Just as He is kind, loving and compassionate to all, so too must we strive to restrain our innate selfishness and subjectivity, emulating His kindness and generosity in the way we look upon and deal with others.

The evil eye against Israel

Bilaam surveyed the orderly Israelite camp in the wilderness, and bursting with jealousy and fury, he sought to curse them eternally - though God did not let him. Similarly, many people around the world today see the tremendous success of modern Israel in science, technology, communications, social welfare and much else, yet instead wondering at God's purpose in elevating this tiny nation to center-stage in world affairs, they can do nothing but find fault in Israel's behavior at every juncture in its precarious existence, endlessly accusing and condemning this nation.

Israel has the highest number of scientists and technicians per capita in the world. It is to Israel that the world owes the first personal computer chips, cellular phones, wireless Internet, voice-technology, instant messaging, many life-saving drugs, the most advanced methods in agriculture, desalinization of sea water, and much else. Taking care of Jews around the world, Israel is the largest immigrant-absorbing nation on earth, while respecting other religions. It is the only country in the Middle East where Christians, Muslims and Jews are all free to vote.

In spite of all of this, all kinds of commentators, lobbyists, activists and other opinion-leaders all over the world would like to see Israel disappear off the face of the earth, even though God has promised that this will never happen.

Looking favorably

The story of Bilaam's evil eye is a moral lesson to all people. Just as God is overflowing with generosity and looks favorably on all, judging everyone positively, so he wants us to do the same.

The outstanding Chassidic luminary, Rabbi Nachman of Breslov (1772-1810) explained how to look favorably on all people - including our own selves!

"**Know** that you must judge all people favorably. This applies even to the worst of people. You must search until you find some little bit of good in them. In that good place inside them, they are not bad! If you can just find this little bit of good and judge them favorably, you really can elevate them and swing the scales of judgment in their favor. This way you can bring them back to God.

You must also find the good in yourself. A fundamental principle in life is that you should always try to keep happy and steer well away from depression. When you start looking deep inside yourself, you may think you have no good in you at all. You may feel you are full of evil, and the negative voice inside you tries to make you depressed. Don't let yourself fall into depression. Search until you find some little good in you. How could it be that you never did anything good in your whole life?

When you start examining your good deed, you may see that it had many flaws. Maybe you did it for the wrong reasons and with the wrong attitude. Even so, how could it be that your good deed contains no good at all? It must contain some element of good.

You must search and search until you find some good point inside yourself to give you new life and make you happy. When you discover the good that is still in you, you genuinely move from being guilty to having merit. Through this you will be able to return to God."

(From Rabbi Nachman's teaching of **Azamra**)

The Covenant of Peace

And God spoke to Moses, saying: 'Pinchas, son of Elazar, son of Aaron the priest has turned away My wrath from the children of Israel, in that he was very jealous among them for My sake, so that I did not consume the children of Israel in My jealousy.

Therefore say: I am hereby giving him My Covenant of Peace; and it shall belong to him and his descendants after him, the covenant of an everlasting priesthood; because he was jealous for his God, and atoned for the children of Israel.'

Numbers 25:10-13

The act for which Pinchas earned God's eternal Covenant of Peace was described in the dramatic closing lines of the previous portion of Balak (Numbers chapter 25, vv. 25:1-9). Having failed to undermine Israel through Bilaam's intended curses, the Moabites sent their daughters and those of the Midianites to seduce the people into idolatry - and succeeded. At the very moment when Moses sought to bring the Israelite perpetrators to justice, Zimri, Prince of the tribe of Shimon, publicly paraded his chosen Midianite courtesan before the entire people, silencing Moses by pointing out that he himself had married a Midianite.

Pinchas alone had the courage to take the initiative, braving a mass lynch by all Zimri's fellow tribesmen and supporters to spear the embracing couple through their sexual organs, thereby saving the entire people of Israel from a ravaging plague sent by God out of anger at this flagrant breach of the code of sexual purity that is very foundation of His law.

It is a Torah principle that if humans here "below" fail to impose justice of their own accord, God Himself unleashes his emissaries from "above" to ensure that justice reigns. But if humans take the initiative to judge themselves and do what is necessary to rectify wrongs and injustice, the need for God to send punishments from "above" is obviated (Midrash Rabbah Deuteronomy, Shoftim 5; Rabbi Nachman Likutey Moharan 1:15). Thus, despite the mass conspiracy to acquiesce in Zimri's blatant immorality, Pinchas knew the truth and publicly avenged it here "below", thereby averting God's vengeance from "above" in the form of the plague.

What is sexual purity?

At the heart of the Torah code of sexual purity is the sanctity of the marital relationship between man and wife, which is protected by the fourth of the Seven Laws of the Children of Noah forbidding a series of sexual prohibitions, including adultery, incest, anal intercourse between men and bestiality. Only a healthy, loving marriage provides the necessary structure within which to breed and raise good, healthy children as the future peace-loving citizens of the earth in accordance with God's commandment to Adam, father of all humanity: "Be fruitful and multiply and fill the earth" (Genesis 1:28).

The sexual drive is one of the most, if not *the* single most powerful of all of our physical drives, and this is our greatest challenge in life. For the sake of the continuity and ever-greater perfection of humanity, God's law invites us to elevate our sexual desires and satisfy them within the framework of a loving marital relationship where physical intimacy becomes the very foundation of the unity of man and wife, finding embodiment in the actual bodies and souls of their children, which are literally built out of a fusion of the seed of both partners.

There would be no great merit in rising to this challenge were it not for the constant contrary temptations to which we are subject to satisfy our sexual desires quickly and easily through mastur-bation, casual, indiscriminate sexual relationships and the like, free of any of the restrictions, responsibilities and burdens that come with marriage.

There was a time when the sanctity of marriage and raising children was respected as a funda-mental value in almost all human societies. Even where extra-marital sexual relationships were rife, they were publicly frowned upon. However, from the late-19th century onwards, Western philosophers and psychologists began to regard traditional morality as repressive and unhealthy, increasingly encouraging people to accept, pursue and flaunt all their sexual urges and desires. The American psychologist Alfred Charles Kinsey (1894-1956) and the German-American philosopher Herbert Marcuse (1898-1979) were among the leading apostles of the new trend, which has reached a point where today sexual license and promiscuity are accepted, promoted and glorified in all the mainstream newspapers and magazines, on TV, in advertising, popular music, films, fashion, sports and even children's education.

For example, 50 years ago the London "Times" was Britain's most modest and self-respecting newspaper compared to the gutter press, printing only a minimum of black-and-white pictures with never a single one showing someone unclad or in any kind of suggestive pose. But today, virtually not a single day goes by without several full-color, sexually-suggestive pictures and adverts appearing on its front page, entertainments, sports, lifestyle, health and fashion sections.

Today anyone of any age who has Internet access or a mobile phone can with a few clicks enter a seemingly endless sub-world extending quite literally across the globe, offering every kind of sexual stimulation, eroticism, pornography, "dating" and other services.

Who is zealous for God?

This total revolution in the surrounding society and culture now enjoys the full protection of the apparatus of secular law in all countries that see themselves as the "freest", most "advanced" and "enlightened", institutionalizing forms of sexual "education" in schools that confer perfect legitimacy upon sexual license and "sensible" promiscuity (i.e. with condoms available from high school dispensers), while at the same time fully equating homosexual relationships with heterosexual marital union, giving them the same social benefits.

Anyone who stands up in public to protest the ubiquitous sexual indecency and permissiveness in the media, entertainment, advertising etc. and in their place to promote sexual and moral purity risks being mocked and ridiculed as a fanatical die-hard extremist who seeks to impose an out-dated, repressive, puritanical code designed to kill people's "freedom".

Yet the gift of God's eternal Covenant of Peace to Pinchas in reward for singlehandedly standing up against the blatant flouting of His law clearly shows the true Torah view of indiscriminate sexual license as against the sanctity of the marital relationship.

In our times, no single leader of the stature of a Pinchas has as yet arisen to quell the tides of sexual immorality and degradation now engulfing our world through the instigation of a mass movement for self-judgment and repair here "below". Accordingly, God Himself has begun to unleash His judgments on the world from "above" - i.e. through some of the many agents that blindly perform His will. On one level, these can be seen to include the sexually-transmitted AIDS virus that has wreaked havoc in our sexually permissive world. On another level, these agents of vengeance might also be seen to include the ever-increasing numbers of distracted, impulsive, violent, demented extremists manifesting in societies all over the world who are dragging us all down into ever-deepening morasses of cyclical corruption, violence and societal disintegration.

We cannot say that we have not been warned.

Do Not Corrupt The Land!

Do not corrupt the land which you are in. For it is blood that corrupts the land; and no expiation can be made for the land for the blood that is shed in it except through the blood of the one that shed it. (Numbers 35:33)

Conclusion of the Book of Numbers

In many years the two concluding portions of the Book of Numbers, known respectively as *Matot* and *Mas'ei*, are both read in the Synagogue on the same Sabbath in order to ensure that the opening portion of Deuteronomy is read on the Sabbath immediately prior to the Fast of the 9th Av commemorating the destruction of the Temple.

The whole of Deuteronomy consists of Moses' closing discourses prior to his death. These were all given in the plains of Moab where Israel were encamped at the end of 40 years of wandering in the wilderness, poised to enter the Promised Land under Joshua, who was already marked out as Moses' successor.

All the later sections of the book of Numbers (from chapter 20 v.14 onwards), including our two present portions, deal with the final period of Israel's sojourn in the Wilderness and their encounters with the various nations that lived around the Promised Land. These included the Edomites to the southeast (Numbers 20:14ff), the Amalekites in the south (Numbers 21:1ff, see Rashi there), the Emorites, from whom Moses conquered territories east of the River Jordan (Numbers 21:21ff), the inhabitants of the region of Bashan to the northeast, whose lands he also conquered (Numbers 21:33ff), and the Moabites and Midianites, who tried to curse and corrupt the people of Israel (Numbers 22:2-25:3).

The first of our two portions, *Matot*, deals with the war of vengeance that God commanded Moses to wage against the Midianites, and with the settlement of the conquered territories of the Emorites and the Bashan region by the tribes of Reuben, Gad and half the tribe of Manasseh.

Our second portion, *Mas'ei*, begins by recounting all the stations of the Israelites' journey from Egypt through the wilderness to the borders of their ancestral land.

After this God instructed Moses as to how the land was to be divided among the remaining nine and a half tribes, defining the exact boundaries of the Promised Land (Numbers 34:1-15) and the names of the tribal chiefs who would preside over the land allocations (Numbers 34:16-27).

The key to civilized living

All-important is the last major section of the book of Numbers, chapter 35, which deals with how the Children of Israel were to live in their land as a "light to the nations".

1. The Levite Cities (Numbers 35:1-8)

Since the Levites were dedicated to service in the Temple and had no single tribal allotment of their own in the land, they were to be given forty-two cities dispersed among all the other tribes, who were commanded to support them with tithes. This would ensure that even when the rest of the people were preoccupied with their day-to-activities making a livelihood etc. an elite of scholars and teachers would be available every-where to teach the people the Torah and how to subject their lives to its wisdom.

2. Cities of Refuge for Unwitting Killers (Numbers 35:9-34)

The Torah contains a complete system for dealing with killers of various kinds, making a clear distinction between unintentional killing and intentional murder.

A human is capable of killing with bare hands, just as animals kill with their "hug" or more often with their teeth or poisonous bite. Just as man is distinguished from all the animals by his use of tools of many different kinds, so too man alone has the power to kill through the use of tools - i.e.

weapons, which are far more deadly than teeth, such as the knife, sword or bullet or other means. Even with no intention to kill, fallible humans using often complex technology that harnesses powerful natural forces can often cause fatal accidents, as in the case of car crashes, domestic and industrial accidents and the like.

Such killings are quite different from intentional murder motivated by hatred, as in the case of the first murder in the Bible, when Cain killed his brother Abel because of jealousy (Genesis 4:8).

The Torah so abhors killing of any kind that even the unintentional killer must move to one of the cities of refuge, strictly segregated from the rest of society, in order to live a life of soul-searching and repentance so as to atone for his negligence.

Most abhorrent of all is intentional murder, which is forbidden under the Seven Noahide Laws. The intentional killer does not deserve to live, and must be executed.

"There is nothing to which the Torah is more opposed than bloodshed, as is written: 'Do not corrupt the land... for it is blood that corrupts the land' (Numbers 35:33)."

Maimonides, Mishneh Torah, Laws of Killing and Protection of Life 1:4

The laws of the penalties for killing and murder are repeated again and again in the Five Books of

Moses. The prohibition of murder is the sixth of the Ten Commandments (Exodus 20:13). The distinction between unintentional killing and murder is made in Exodus 21:12-14. The death penalty for murder is given in Leviticus 24:17. The cities of refuge, judicial procedure and the penalty for murder are dealt with at length in our present portion of *Mas'ei* in Numbers 35: 9-34, and again, also at some length, in Deuteronomy 19:1-13.

The Death Penalty

The only killing that is sanctioned in the Torah is in legitimate warfare against sworn enemies who refuse the call to peace (Deuteronomy 20:10) and against terrorists (=Amalek, Deuteronomy 25:19), and judicial killing for specific crimes, especially murder.

The Torah clearly and unequivocally requires the death penalty for the intentional killer. Moreover the Torah teaches that it is precisely the failure to impose the death penalty that corrupts the land: **"For it is blood that corrupts the land, and no expiation can be made for the land for the blood that is shed in it except through the blood of the one that shed it"** (Numbers 35:33).

Some people are under the mistaken apprehension that Torah law is lenient to the killer on account of the apparent requirement that a murder must have been duly witnessed by two valid witnesses in order for the murderer to be executed (Numbers

35:30). They infer that in most cases, murderers could never be executed for their crimes.

This is wrong, as clearly stated by Rabbi Moses ben Maimon (Maimonides) in his authoritative Code of Torah Law:

In the case of all murderers who are not technically liable to the death penalty at the hands of the rabbinical court, if the legitimate government wants to have them executed under state law for the welfare of the world, they are entitled to do so. Likewise, if the rabbinical court saw fit to execute them as an emergency measure if the circumstances justify this, they are entitled to do as they see fit.

Maimonides, Mishneh Torah, Laws of Killing and Protection of Life 2:4

"The compassion of the wicked is cruel" (Proverbs 12:10)

45 years ago as a boy of 15, I sat in the visitors' gallery of the British House of Commons during the debate on the suspension of capital punishment for murder, which was implemented in 1965, followed by the complete abolition of capital punishment in 1969.

As an impressionable teenager, it was easy to be swayed by the eloquent arguments of the abolitionists in the name of enlightened compassion. Today, nearly half a century later, the consequences of their misplaced compassion may be seen in the culture of guns, knives and violence that has taken hold of Britain, as in so many other "enlightened" and "advanced" countries. Fifty years ago, murders and violent attacks were very rare and single cases occupied the attention of the media for weeks. Today the stabbings and shootings follow one another so fast that they are quickly overtaken by each ensuing outrage.

There is no deterrence against murder when the killer knows that he will never be in fear of losing his own life. At worst, if caught and convicted, he will live out his days enjoying the free hospitality of a taxpayer-financed prison that provides him with a variety of enjoyable physical recreation and other facilities, TV and entertainment, the ability to study, etc. with no worries about ever being unemployed or going hungry. In many cases convicted killers have excellent prospects of having their sentences remitted to little more than a few years.

This is one of the main reasons for the endless series of shootings, knifings and violent attacks that are reported every single day, which are also encouraged by the incessant diet of killing and violence provided by TV, films and fiction.

Many people who consider themselves highly enlightened imagine that all the world already recognizes how evil it is to kill, and they argue that this being so, the death penalty for killers must also be immoral. Even where they accept that criminal murderers should at least be locked up for their crimes, their "liberalism" makes them take a lenient view of killings perpetrated by those they view as "freedom fighters" seeking to overturn corrupt, tyrannical regimes. Thus "enlightened" and "compassionate" liberals throughout the world tend to turn a blind eye to or even justify killings and other forms of violence perpetrated by those who in their political lexicon are on the side of "good", while vilifying any kind of violence by those they see as being on the side of "evil".

Accordingly, worldwide censure of Israel for using "disproportionate violence" in handling the many security risks to which they are exposed goes hand in hand with a lenient and even favorable view of actual fomenters of violence and adulators of bloodshed all over the world.

Scarcely a day goes by without reports of mass-casualty terrorist attacks by "Moslems" against "Moslems", eliciting little more than a sigh. On the very day I am writing these words, over 50 have been killed in the latest attacks in Baghdad, Iraq, including 32 targeted in a suicide bombing at a revered Shiite religious shrine. On the same day the media are reporting that the Al Qaeda terror network has launched an English language Internet site including articles like "Make a bomb in the kitchen of your mother".

The British-Pakistan author and historian Tariq Ali has characterized the state religion of Saudi Arabia - birthplace of Al Qaeda - as being "not an everyday version of Sunni or Shia Islam but a peculiarly virulent, ultra-puritanical strain known as Wahhabism. an artificially manufactured denomination of Islam which authorizes the killing of Shiite Muslims as a means of entering heaven". If it is permissible to kill fellow Muslims, how much more is the killing of non-Muslims esteemed. But the multi-million dollar oil, defense and other interests shared by Saudi Arabia with the "enlightened" countries of America, Britain and Europe etc. stand in the way of any meaningful protests by the latter.

The killers and the liberals

The ideology of terror legitimizes random killings of innocent men, women and children without trial in the name of some religious-political "war against evil".

This is completely contrary to the teaching of the Torah, which demands due judicial procedure in all cases, as we see in the section on killing in our portion of *Mas'ei*. Proper judicial procedure including thorough investigations are required even in the case of a city that has reverted to idolatry (Deut. 13:13-19). No group of terrorists or anyone else is ever allowed to take the law into their own hands because of what they imagine to be morally justified.

But today the terrorists and their state backers and supporters are in the ascendant. They are delighted that the "compassionate liberals" of the "enlightened countries" have gone soft on killing, since this simply advances their agenda.

The world is in danger of descending ever-deeper into a horrendous chasm of violence, bloodshed and barbarity.

The only hope for civilization is to return to the wisdom of the Torah:

No expiation can be made for the land for the blood that is shed in it except through the blood of the one that shed it (Numbers 35:33).

Lands and Their Owners

Structure of the book of Deuteronomy

The entire book of Deuteronomy consists of Moses' discourses to the people of Israel in the concluding weeks of his life. The people were encamped in the Plains of Moab, poised to enter their ancestral land. The earlier sections of the book (especially from Deuteronomy 3:23-11:25) mainly review the basic foundations of faith, belief, love and fear of God, awareness of the Exodus and Sinaitic Covenant upon which Israel's global mission is based. The central sections (Deut. 11:26-26:15) give a detailed exposition of the laws that are to rule all aspects of their lives, including the Temple, judiciary, government, marriage, divorce, domestic, business and social life. The closing discourses (from Deut. 26:16 until the end of the book) give Moses' final reproof to the people and his warnings and blessings before his death.

An Historical Excursus

In the present opening portion of the book of Deuteronomy, which is called by the same Hebrew name as the whole book - **Devarim** - Moses prefaces these final discourses with an extensive historical excursus reviewing some key aspects of

Israel's journey through the wilderness to their Land, paying special attention to their encounters and relations with the peoples who dwelled in the neighboring territories, especially Edom (descendants of Isaac's son Esau), Moab and Ammon (descendants of Abraham's nephew, Lot; Deuteronomy 2:2-23).

God forbade Israel to provoke Edom: "For I will not give you of their land, not so much as for the sole of the foot to tread upon; because I have given Mount Seir to Esau for a possession" (Deut. 2:5). The same applied to Moab: "For I will not give you of their land as an inheritance, for I have given Ar to the children of Lot for a possession" (ibid. v. 9). The same also applied to Ammon: "For I will not give you from the land of the children of Ammon for an inheritance, for I have given it to the children of Lot as an inheritance" (ibid. v. 19).

In the course of this section the Torah mentions a variety of indigenous peoples that had previously inhabited those territories (Deut. chapter 2 vv. 10-12 & 20-23), noting how Children of Esau and the Children of Moab usurped and destroyed the original dwellers in their respective lands (vv. 12 and 22). They were able to do so because "God destroyed them before them and they succeeded them and dwelt in their stead" (v. 21).

"The Earth is the Lord's" (Psalms 24:1)

The Torah teaches us that the various peoples of the world own and dwell in their lands - or may be dispossessed from them - only because "the Most High gave to the nations their inheritance, He separated the children of men, He set the borders of the peoples." (Deuteronomy 32:8).

The Five Books of Moses must indeed be seen as the oldest deed of land ownership in the world. God gave the Land of Israel to Abraham, Isaac and Jacob and their descendants forever. The Torah defines the exact boundaries of this (Genesis 15:18-21 and Numbers 34:1-12), stipulating that the essential condition for Israel's ownership is observance of God's commandments (Deuteronomy 11:13-17 etc.).

It is the very height of irony that today, practically all the nations of the world as represented in the United Nations and other international organizations are engaged in a concerted campaign contesting the legitimacy of the Jewish national homeland in Israel's ancestral territories. However, this is not a new phenomenon. Nearly a thousand years ago, Rashi, prince of the Torah commentators (Rabbi Shlomo Yitzhaki 1040-1105), opened his commentary on Genesis by explaining that the Torah itself is the answer to this challenge:

"'He has declared to His people the power of His works, in giving them the heritage of the nations' (Psalms 111:6). For if the nations of the world say to Israel, 'You are robbers because you conquered the lands of the seven (Canaanite) nations', they say to them: 'All the earth belongs to the Holy One blessed-be-He; He created it and gave it to who-ever was fit in His eyes; through His favor He gave it to them and through His favor He took it from them and gave it to us'" (Rashi on Genesis 1:1).

Conquests and occupations

Practically the whole of human history is the story of the occupation of lands by various ethnic groups and their subsequent conquest and occupation by other groups.

When the Children of Noah first began to spread in all directions across the world, they consisted of tiny family groups and clans that discovered vast expanses of lands of every kind ready for them to take, conquer from nature and develop. In the case of ownerless land and the resources it contains, Torah law explicitly grants ownership to the first comer (Maimonides, Mishneh Torah, Laws of Property Rights and Gifts 1:1).

As populations grew and developed in different ways, various groups were frequently tempted to try to improve their lives by migrating to better territories, which they often conquered from their previous inhabitants, whom they either drove out or enslaved. The Bible itself records some of the history of such conquests, such as those of the Edomites and Moabites recounted in our present portion of **Devarim** (see above). The Book of Kings, Daniel, Ezra and Nehemiah, Esther etc. trace the rise and fall of the great ancient "world" empires of Assyria, Babylon, the Medes and Persians, under which enormous tracts of lands were seized from their native inhabitants, who were often forcibly deported. The Persian Empire was defeated by Alexander the Great, and the Greek Empire was then superseded by the Roman Empire.

In the "Dark Ages" various different "barbarians" spread in many directions. Britain was conquered by the Angles and Saxons, and then by the Normans. The last five hundred and more years since the "discovery" of America by Christopher Columbus witnessed unparalleled conquests of territories throughout the world by European powers such as Britain, Holland, France, Italy and Spain. It was normal practice for the colonial powers to plunder the lands and resources they conquered and either enslave the indigenous peoples or consign them to lives of inferiority, disenfranchisement and poverty.

The European colonial empires have officially been dismantled, yet Britain continues to occupy Northern Ireland and also regards the far-off Falkland Islands as its territory. British forces are currently operating side by side with American and other NATO forces in Iraq and Afghanistan, even though these countries are thousands of miles from their own countries. Turkey occupies large parts of Kurdistan even though the Turks and Kurds are ethnically different. China occupies Tibet even though the Tibetans are a different people. Russia occupies parts of Chechnya and Georgia, Spain and France occupy the Basque country, the United States of America occupies the lands of the indigenous American Indians.

Legitimate business

Our portion of **Devarim** teaches that while Israel were authorized to conquer the territories that God promised to the patriarchs, they were forbidden to conquer the land of the Edomites since this was not part of God's gift. On the contrary, they were explicitly commanded to conduct themselves towards them in a civil manner, buying any food supplies they needed on their way, including even the basic necessity of water, for which they were to pay ready money (Deuteronomy 2:6).

From this we learn that even where the national aspirations of one nation are different from those of another, they must not regard one another as objects for conquest and plunder. On the contrary, they must relate to one another peacefully, buying or selling in order to benefit one another.

Know Today...

Know today, and bring it into your heart that HaShem, He is God in heaven above and upon the earth beneath; there is none else (Deuteronomy 4:39).

In our present portion of **Va-etchanan**, Moses launches into the main body of his final discourses to Israel and the world, which he starts by reviewing the very fundamentals of faith in God and the way we are to serve Him through the practice of His commandments.

The foundation of the entire edifice is contained in the key verse:

Know today, and bring it into your heart that HaShem, He is God in heaven above and upon the earth beneath; there is none else (Deuteronomy 4:39).

It greatly behooves us to ponder the true meaning and implications of this precept, which is set forth by the outstanding codifier of Torah law, **Ra**bbi **M**oshe **b**en **M**aimon ("Rambam", Moses Maimonides 1135-1204), in the opening words of his great Code:

The foundation of foundations and the pillar of all kinds of wisdom is to know that there exists a First Existent, and it is He that brings into being every existent, and all that exists in heaven and on earth and what is between them exists only through the truth of His existence.

Maimonides, Mishneh Torah, Foundations of the Torah (*Yesodey HaTorah*) 1:1

Know today.

What is this knowledge that we are commanded to cultivate? How is it possible for humans in any sense to attain "knowledge" of the Living God, who is infinite and all-powerful? We cannot even gaze directly at the sun without getting blinded. The sun is merely one of God's creations - how then could we presume to sneak a look at G-d and know Him?

It is obviously impossible to "know" God in the same way that we know any of His creations - through our five physical senses and our rational faculties - because God has no knowable form and entirely transcends the physical, material world. Nor is the knowledge of God that we must seek mere mental knowledge and understanding of some basic axiom that is inherently no different from any of the other axioms of rational thought, such as the truism that 2+2=4. Once having once learned such axioms, we know them for all time without needing constantly to advance and deepen our understanding of them.

But Moses says, "Know **today**" - i.e. every single day of our lives - and he adds immediately that we must also **bring it into our heart**. We are being asked to do more than simply know in our minds that there exists a First Cause. Mere intellectual cognition of this fundamental axiom of all axioms is not sufficient. We must bring this knowledge **into our hearts** - into our awareness on all levels and into our innermost being. The "heart" is not only the physical organ that ceaselessly pumps blood around our bodies as long as we are alive. The "heart" is an expression for the seat of all our knowledge, awareness, feelings, emotions and intuitions. The heart is the very center of our being - the **self**. Thus we are commanded to bring the knowledge of God into ourselves until this knowledge permeates and transforms every part of our being.

This is not a one-time task that once performed may be left aside. We must know God **today** - because we can never attain final, ultimate knowledge of God. We must constantly go forward and advance in our apprehensions. Our knowledge of God must constantly develop and unfold with every passing day. We must strive to increase our knowledge and understanding of God every single day and at every moment.

Concealment

If what we have to know and believe were so clear and obvious at all times, there would be no need for a specific precept and commandment constantly to increase our awareness and understanding. It is precisely because it is **not** always clear and obvious that we are obliged to make constant efforts to advance and deepen our knowledge of God, gaining ever-renewed apprehension of what is ultimately intrinsically unfathomable.

From the beginnings of human history, people of all races, backgrounds and beliefs have known that divine forces rule the world in which we find ourselves - the earth and its surrounding planets and stars. All people also have an underlying awareness that sovereign over all these forces is the one supreme Power that we call God.

Yet it is perfectly possible to look at and ponder existence and imagine that the universe is nothing more than a random concatenation of subatomic forces having no ultimate purpose or meaning. This indeed is the banner of the modern, purportedly "science-based" doctrines of atheism that are today being ever more aggressively trumpeted by all kinds of highly respected, celebrated "thinkers", "professors", "scientists" and media personalities.

One of the foundations of Torah faith is that God purposely designed a universe that is capable of being construed and interpreted in different ways - either as a most wondrous divine creation or as nothing but a meaningless, freak chance. God did this in order to provide humanity with the challenge of having to search out the real truth through our own efforts, thereby meriting a reward when we discover it.

HASHEM, He is God.

The Hebrew name which in the English biblical translations of our key verse is rendered as "God" is **Elohim**. This is one of the main Hebrew divine names found in the Bible. It appears all through the account of Creation (Genesis chapter 1) and constantly recurs throughout the rest of the Five Books of Moses and the Prophets and Holy Writings (TaNaCh).

The name **Elohim** is grammatically a plural form. Not only is it one of the main Hebrew names referring to the True God. It is also frequently used in the Bible in reference to "other gods", i.e. the objects of idolatry. These "other gods" may indeed be personifications of actual divine powers (such as Venus, goddess of love and fertility, or Mars, god of power, military prowess, etc.). However, the very essence of the Sinaitic Covenant that God struck with Israel for the benefit of all humanity is that all these different powers exist only in virtue of the One Supreme Almighty God who created everything and rules over all.

In our verse, Moses is teaching us that the thing that we have to know when we encounter such a vast diversity of powers and phenomena revealed throughout creation on all the different levels, is that everything comes forth from HaShem.

HaShem

The Hebrew word HaShem simply means "the Name". The word HaShem does not appear in the biblical text of our verse. The Hebrew divine name that is actually written in the Torah scroll is that transliterated in the letters YHVH. This is known as the "essential" name of God. On account of its supreme sanctity, it is strictly forbidden to pronounce it as spelled, and it may not be defaced or erased once it has been written. To avoid possible desecration of this Name, it is customary to refer to it as HaShem.

It was the revelation of this "essential" name of God that was the essence of His self-revelation to Israel at Sinai (Exodus 20:2, cf. Exodus 6:2-3). In our key verse, Moses is saying that the very essence of what we must strive to know and understand ever more deeply with every new day and moment in our lives is that "HaShem, He is God".

What we are to know is that, underlying all the diverse phenomena that we experience in so many different ways, day after day, moment after moment, there is one single, sovereign Power. We are constantly exposed to different experiences. Our entire purpose and mission in ever-changing circumstances is to uncover and make ourselves aware of the unifying factor, the ultimate Divine unity that underlies everything.

Some believe in a supreme God but imagine that He is remote and unreachable "in Heaven", as if He set the universe in motion like a master craftsman who made a watch, only to withdraw and leave the world to its own devices, neither knowing nor caring what goes on here on earth.

This is not true. Moses is teaching us that we are to know and understand that God is not only in Heaven "up there", but also right here with us on earth "down below". God is present in everything and rules over everything. Indeed, the essential mission of Abraham and his true heirs is to bring this knowledge to the world (See Rashi on Genesis 24:7). And in order to bring it to others, we must first bring it into our own hearts.

This knowledge leads to the ultimate joy, because the Torah teaches that God is good - perfect goodness - and therefore ultimately everything is for good, including even pain, suffering and death.

Know today, and bring it into your heart that HaShem, He is God in heaven above and upon the earth beneath; there is none else (Deuteronomy 4:39).

Readings from Rabbi Nachman on Faith and Knowledge of God

Know it in your heart

"Know this day and consider it in your heart that HaShem is God in heaven above and on earth below; there is no other" (Deuteronomy 4:39).

The only way to know God is through complete faith. Only faith can bring you to true knowledge and perception of God's greatness: "And I will betroth you to Me with faith, and you shall know God!" (Hosea 2:22).

Many passages tell us to know God: "Know this day and consider it in your heart... "(Deuteronomy 4:39)."Know the God of your father" (I Chronicles 28:9)."Know that HaShem is God" (Psalms 100:3). These verses teach us to know and be mindful of God's presence at all times and not to forget Him for a moment.

Great kings constantly remind their subjects that they have a ruler. Soldiers in particular are trained to know who their king and master is - "In order that His fear should be on their faces" (Exodus 20:17) - so that they should serve their master unconditionally. Subordinates are constantly told, "Know that you have a lord and master." The intention is that they should keep this in mind and never forget it, in order not do anything against his will.

The same is true of the Kingdom of Heaven. We are told: "Know the God of your father!" Know it and don't ever forget it! "Know this day and consider it in your heart, that HaShem is God!" "Know that HaShem is God!"

We need to be reminded time and time again. Everyone knows in general terms that "HaShem is God". However, the distractions and temptations of this vain world cause many to forget it much of the time. This is why the Torah reminds us: "Know that HaShem is God!" "Know the God of your father!" That is to say: Bring this knowledge deep within yourself until it is bound tightly in your mind and heart at all times. This is the meaning of "Know this day and consider it in your heart that HaShem is God."

Perfect knowledge is when you bind your mind to your heart so that you know in your heart that "HaShem is God." When you bring this knowledge into your heart, you will be filled with deep awe, fear and reverence of God and you will not sin.

Each person's knowledge and awareness of God are unique to himself according to the horizons of his heart. Our basic knowledge of God derives from what we have been taught by our holy forefathers, who struggled all their lives to divest themselves of all material attachments. They conquered all their negative traits and desires, releasing themselves from the root of evil. This was how they came to a true recognition and understanding of their Creator.

They have left this good heritage to us and our duty is to accept it with the utmost joy. "Happy are we! How good is our portion! How pleasant is our lot! How beautiful is our heritage!" (Morning Prayers).

When the Torah tells us to "know" God, it is teaching us to bring this holy knowledge into our minds and thoughts and bind it in our hearts constantly at all times in order that "His fear will be upon our faces so that we will not sin" (Exodus 20:17).

Sichot Haran #217

Knowing God

It is impossible to explain to someone else how you personally perceive God's greatness. You can't even explain it to yourself from one day to the next. Tomorrow you will not be able to recapture completely the understanding you had today.

It is impossible to describe one's perceptions of God. They are so lofty - higher than high! They cannot be put into words.

Sichot Haran #1

The goal of knowledge: to know that we know nothing

The ultimate goal of all knowledge of God is to realize that one knows nothing. Yet even this is unattainable. A person may come to realize his own ignorance, but only in a certain area on a particular level. There is still the next level, which he has not even touched. He does not know enough about the next level to begin to realize his ignorance. No matter how high he climbs, there is always the next step. A person therefore knows nothing: he cannot even understand his own ignorance. For there will always be a level of ignorance beyond his present level of perception.

Sichot Haran #3

* * *

The more you draw yourself to God, the more you must realize how far you are from Him. When a person believes that he has succeeded in achieving closeness to God and understanding of Him, it is a sign that he does not know anything at all. If he did, he would understand that he is very far from God and knows absolutely nothing, because God's greatness is without limits.

Likutey Moharan I, 63

* * *

Hints, messages and guidance

You should reflect on the different situations and occurrences that God sends your way day by day. Each day has its own thoughts, words and deeds. They are all completely unique to that day. God "contracts" His infinite, endless Godliness in such a way that Godliness is present even in the innermost point of the finite material world in which man finds himself. Thus God sends to each individual the thoughts, words and deeds appropriate for the day, the person and the place. Within them are hints intended to draw the person closer to God's service.

This is why you should pay attention to what happens to you and consider what it may signify. Think about the thoughts, words and deeds that God sends you each day in order to understand His hints to you to draw closer to Him at every moment. This applies to everyone, no matter who and in what circumstances.

But be cautious when thinking about these things: you must stay within certain limits and not delve to excess, because otherwise it is possible to stray beyond the bounds of holiness. Flying off into speculation can be dangerous. Stay within the limits of human understanding and steadily expand your horizons without trying to step beyond your level, because "you may not investigate that which is too wondrous for you" (Chagigah 13a).

Likutey Moharan I, 54

* * *

God is in everything

The whole earth is full of God's glory. No place is devoid of God, Who fills all the worlds and transcends all the worlds.

Therefore, even one whose occupation involves contact with non-believers cannot excuse himself from serving God on account of being constantly surrounded by gross materialism. Godliness can be found everywhere, in all material things and even in the languages of the nations. Without Godliness they could not exist or endure at all. It is just that as the levels descend, Godliness becomes increasingly "contracted" and veiled in many garments.

Accordingly, even if you are sunk in the very lair of evil on the lowest of all levels, even if you believe you are so far from God that it is impossible for you to draw closer, you can still find Godliness in the very place to which you have sunk. There too you can attach yourself to Him and repent with all your heart. Even there, God is not far away. It is just that the veils are thicker.

Likutey Moharan I, 33

* * *

God's glory cries out from all things, for "The whole earth is filled with His glory" (Isaiah 6:3). Even the stories of the nations cry out with God's glory: "Let the nations tell of His glory!" (Psalms 96:3). His glory is reflected even in their tales and stories.

God's glory cries out, calling and signaling you to draw closer. For God wants you with all His love and kindness.

Sometimes your prayers become like flames and the words flow from your lips with burning fervor and desire. This is God's own light within you, calling you to draw near. Your fervent passion is a spark of God's own essence - for "He is your praise, He is your God" (Deuteronomy 10:21). God Himself is your praise and prayer. Sometimes you can literally pray before God Himself.

And even when God withdraws and seems far away, you must still pray to Him. You must actually cast your prayers, throwing them towards God from afar, as it says: "Cast your burden upon God" (Psalms 55:23). "Happy is the man who knows how to cast arrows" (Tikkuney Zohar). These "arrows" are the prayers that must be thrown towards God.

Sichot Haran #52

Wisdom for life

This world exists only to bring about God's eternal purpose.

There is no need to be upset about whether or not you have money. Even with money, you could waste away your days. The world deceives us completely. It makes us think we are constantly gaining but we end up with nothing. People spend years working to make money, but in the end, when they come to the final reckoning, they are left with nothing in their hands. Even when someone becomes rich, in the end he is taken from his money.

Man and wealth cannot remain together. Either the money is taken from the man or the man from his money. No- one has ever stayed with his money. Where is all the money people have been making since the beginning of time? People have always been busy making money - so where is all the money? It has all become absolutely nothing!

Who can say that he serves God according to God's true greatness? Someone who has even the faintest conception of God's greatness cannot understand how anyone could claim to serve Him. Even the highest angel cannot boast that he is able to serve God.

The main thing is desire. Always long and yearn to come closer to God.

Many people would like to serve God but not all have the same desire. There are many different levels of desire. Even in one and the same person, the intensity of his desire may change from moment to moment. The main thing is to yearn constantly for God - and in between, to pray, study and keep His commandments.

Nor is there any need for sophistication. Just be sincere and simple. Even in your sincerity, you must not be foolish. But sophistication is totally unnecessary.

It is no good to be old. Whether it's an old Chassid or an old Tzaddik, being old is no good. Be new each day. Always make a fresh start. The only thing that improves with age is a pig, which becomes stronger as it grows older (Shabbat 77b).

Nor is there any need to be extreme. Serving God is not fanaticism. The real fanatics are those who pursue the material world without serving God. People consider it fanatical when a person completely abandons the material world to immerse himself wholly in devotion. Yet even this is unnecessary. You can serve God without going to extremes.

Take my advice and don't let the world fool you. No-one ever came to a good end by pursuing worldliness. Even those who hold the entire world in their hands end up badly, losing out both in themselves and for generations to come.

If the world is nothing, what can you do? To know what to do in this world you need help from Heaven. But as the people of Israel, we need no further help. We already know what we must do, because the Torah teaches us what to do.

People say you should not seek greatness, but I say you should seek only greatness. Look for the greatest possible Tzaddik. Choose only the greatest Tzaddik as your teacher.

The passions that wear man down do not really exist. We have to eat and drink and do what is necessary to sustain the body. Likewise, we must have children. All this is necessary, and can be accomplished in holiness and purity.

Man's mind has the power to withstand all temptations. Every person has the potential of wisdom. You must bring out this potential wisdom and make it actual. With this potential wisdom alone you can overcome all temptations.

You may have succumbed to the desires of this world and sinned in many ways. You may have damaged your mind, leaving it weak and confused. But you still have some intelligence. With this alone you can overcome all desires. One grain of intelligence can stand against the whole world and all its temptations. Wherever you are, you can be close to God. You can approach God and serve Him even in the lowest pit of hell.

It needs tremendous effort, or help from God - or both - in order to subdue the impurities in the mind until you want nothing in this world and everything is the same to you. Then, "When you walk it will lead you, when you lie down it will watch over you, and when you wake up, it will comfort you" (Proverbs 6:22).

When you have purified your mind, there is no difference between this world, the grave, and the next world. When you only desire God and His Torah, all are the same. In all three you can be attached to God and his Torah.

However, if you are attached to this world, there is an agonizing difference. This world is spread before you while the grave is tight and narrow. But when you purify your mind, all will be the same.

Sichot Haran #51

The good life

The non-believers have no life even in this world. As soon as things go against them, and certainly when trouble strikes, they simply have nowhere to turn. Since they attribute everything to nature, they are left with nothing to fortify them.

But one who has faith and believes in God has a very good life. Even when trouble strikes, he can still fortify himself with his trust in God, because he knows that everything is for the best. Either this suffering will cleanse him of his sins or eventually bring him some great benefit. For God's intention is certainly for good. Therefore, the man of faith always has a good life both in this world and the next.

The non-believers, however, have no life either in this world or the next. Those who really know them see that they are always racked with suffering. They endure constant pain and anxiety because things never go exactly as they want. All their days are filled with pain and anger.

In this world it is impossible for everything to go the way one wants it. Those who ignore the true, enduring purpose of life, satisfying only their material desires, are doomed to a life of constant pain and suffering without having any way to console themselves.

But if you have true faith, your main hope is in the world to come and you therefore have a very good life. Whatever happens to you, you have faith that everything is for good - whether it comes to remind you to repent or to atone for your sins so that you may be worthy of the everlasting good of the world to come.

Your sins and wrongdoing may cause you great anguish. You may suffer the worst agonies of regret. Yet your very contrition over your sins actually increases your days and adds to your life, for "The fear of God increases one's days" (Proverbs 10:27).

You may experience great pain when you regret your sins. You may feel deeply ashamed when contemplating God's exalted greatness. You may cringe in fear of punishment. Whatever form it takes, this suffering is caused by your very fear of God, and "The fear of God increases one's days." Your very pain and anxiety add to your days.

If you are a person of faith, you will find it easier to repent. True repentance must balance the sin. You have to endure pain and suffering in equal measure to the enjoyment derived from the sin.

Since you believe in God, you will never be able to have complete enjoyment from any sin because any wrong you do will be with mixed feelings and in the full knowledge that it will end bitterly. You know the bitter punishment for each sin, so that if you succumb to temptation you are filled with regrets even as you sin. It is therefore much easier for you to repent because you do not have to endure unbearable pangs of repentance since the pleasure from your sin was never very great.

For the non-believers, however, repentance is more of a burden. Having suffered little pain or remorse at the time of the sin, they are obliged to suffer when they repent in order to balance the pleasure of the sin.

Sichot Haran #102

One precious day

"Repent one day before your death" (Avot 2:10).

Yesterday and tomorrow are man's downfall. Today you may be aroused towards God. Don't let yourself become discouraged because of what may have happened yesterday or what may happen tomorrow.

No matter where a person stands, there are always reverses. Many people become discouraged as a result, and stop putting any real effort into their devotions.

That is why you must "Repent one day before your death."

"Before your death" is your entire life. During your entire lifetime, you may be worthy of only one day of repentance.

This one day is more precious than all treasures. For what does a person gain from all his worldly effort? Nothing remains of your entire life other than this one day when you return to God.

Sichot Haran #288

Now!

"Today if you will but listen to His voice!"
(Psalms 95:7).

Think only about the present day and the present moment. When someone wants to serve God, he may see it as a heavy burden. But if you remember that you have only today, it won't be such a burden. Don't push off serving God from one day to the next, saying, "I'll start tomorrow - tomorrow I'll pray with real devotion."

All we have is the present day and the present moment. Tomorrow is a whole different world.

"Today if you will but listen to His voice!" (Psalms 95:7). Today!!!

Likutey Moharan I, 272

TODAY!!!

Man's world consists only of the present. Whatever you can do to serve God, do immediately and determinedly without delay.

Chayey Moharan #431

Please and Thank You

"For not on bread alone does man live but on all that comes forth from the mouth of God will man live."
Deuteronomy 8:3

"Eat and be satisfied and bless HaShem your God."
Deuteronomy 8:10

In our present portion of **Eikev** the Torah teaches us to bless and thank God for the food we eat. "Eat and be satisfied and bless HaShem your God" (Deuteronomy 8:10).

According to tradition, Moses instituted that after eating their food, the Children of Israel should bless God with the "Grace after meals".

Blessed are You, HaShem our God, who sustains the entire universe through His goodness, with grace, with mercy and with kindness. He gives bread to all flesh, for His kindness is forever. And through His great goodness we never have lacked sustenance, and so may we never lack sustenance for ever and ever, for the sake of His great Name. For He is the God Who nourishes and sustains all, and Who is good to all, and Who prepares sustenance for all His creations that He has created. Blessed are You HaShem, Who sustains all.

The Torah sages also taught that if we are to bless God when we are satisfied after having eaten, how much more should we bless God while still hungry - i.e. before eating - in order to acknowledge that He is the ultimate source of our sustenance. Ezra and the Men of the Great Assembly laid down a series of blessings to be recited before eating bread and other baked goods, before drinking wine, eating the fruits of a tree, vegetables and other kinds of food.

Each of these blessings begins with the words: **Blessed are you, HaShem, our God, Ruler of the Universe.**

Over bread, continue: **...Who brings forth bread from the earth.**

Where other foods are eaten with bread, no further blessing is said.

When not eating bread:

Over other baked grain products, continue: **...Who creates varieties of sustenance.**

Over wine, continue: **...Who creates the fruit of the vine.**

Over fruits of trees, continue: **...Who creates the fruit of the tree.**

Over vegetables etc. continue: **...Who creates the fruit of the earth.**

Over other kinds of foods (meat, fish, eggs, cheese, candy, etc.) water and other beverages, we continue: **...through Whose word everything came about.**

Just as these blessings are recited by the people of Israel, so they may be recited by all gentiles.

The simplest of all the blessings is an ancient formula that can be taught to and recited even by little children:

Blessed is the Loving One, Ruler of the World, Master of this bread.

Why are blessings so important?

We are all made with a physical body combined with a spiritual soul that vitalizes the body as long as we are alive in this world. In order to survive, we must meet the many demands and imperatives of the body - for air, food, drink, clothing, housing and so much more. God's will is for us to bring our material side under the control of the spiritual soul, satisfying our needs lawfully and in moderation, using the material world in the service of God through harnessing our physical bodies in the practice of His Torah.

Eating our food is among our most basic physical functions. God's gift of the air we constantly breathe is everywhere freely available – ideally, we should bless God with every breath we take! But food is something that mankind has always had to work for in one way or another, whether through hunting, cultivating the land and other kinds of food production, or by working to earn the money to purchase what others have produced. King Solomon said: "All man's labor is for his mouth" (Ecclesiastes 6:7).

After working very hard for our living, it is easy when sitting to enjoy the fruits of our labors to think to ourselves: "*My* power and the strength of *my* hand has made for me all this prosperity" (Deuteronomy 8:17). Particularly in the hyper-sophisticated technological world in which we live, as we consume the various attractively-packaged ready-made products we have picked from the shelves of the supermarket, it is easy to forget that the manufacturers could never have created any of them without the God-given sunshine, air, water, minerals and incredible diversity of life-forms from which they derive. Rarely if ever does a single product label or advertisement remind us of this!

Consciousness-raising

As we take a piece of food to eat, the brief pause we make in order to bless God for it before taking the first bite is an exercise in consciousness-raising. The blessing may be said aloud, in a whisper or sung with a happy tune. What is important that, after all the work and effort that went into producing and acquiring this food, we remind ourselves that it is ultimately HaShem our God, Ruler of the Universe, Who created and provided us with this very apple, this cup of tea, this bread, this cookie.

And after having eaten and drunk our fill, when we bless and thank God for His kindness and mercy in sustaining us and all the world, we are transmuting our physical, animalistic function of eating into something spiritual, deepening and enhancing our awareness of God's constant presence in every detail of our lives.

When we bless and thank God before and after we eat and drink, the words of our lips bring blessing into our lives and into our very bodies.

"And you shall serve HaShem your God, and He will bless your bread and your water, and I shall remove illness from within you" (Exodus 23:25).

Investigate Diligently

The first three portions of the book of Deuteronomy may be seen as the introductory section of Moses' closing discourses to Israel prior to his death. The main focus of this section, which we concluded in last week's portion, is on the fundamentals of faith, love and fear of God.

In our present portion of **Re'eh**, Moses embarks upon a detailed review and exposition of the entire Torah law code. This continues in the two following portions and the first section of the third (up to Deut. 26:15), after which Moses gives his closing reproofs, warnings and blessings, which take up the remainder of Deuteronomy.

The central pillar of the entire Torah code is "to know that there exists the First Existent, and He brought into being all that exists, and all the existents in the heavens and on earth and all that is in between exist only in virtue of His existence." (Maimonides, Mishneh Torah, Foundations of the Torah, 1:1). To know HaShem is the first of the Ten Commandments (Exodus 20:2).

The second commandment is the logical corollary of the first: All idolatry - the worship of any of HaShem's creations, be it an angel, sphere, star, or any other created being - is prohibited, even if the worshipper knows that HaShem is the God and intends to serve this created being as if to give honor to HaShem (Exodus 20:3-5; Maimonides, Laws of Idolatry 2:1; see Torah for the Nations commentary on Ki Tisa, Exodus 30:11, 34:35. Idolatry and the Power of Repentance.)

The prohibition of idolatry

It is with the strict prohibition against idolatry that Moses begins his exposition of the Torah code in our portion, which contains several different commandments aimed at destroying all relics of idolatry and preventing it from taking root.

1. On entry into their land, Israel were to destroy completely all idolatrous sites, altars, monuments and graven images (Deut. 12:2-3). In their own land, the people of Israel are commanded to pursue and destroy all traces of idolatry, but they are not enjoined to do so in other lands (Maimonides, Laws of Idolatry 7:1).

2. It is forbidden to inquire how idolaters worship their gods so as not to imitate them and thereby become ensnared (Deut. 12:30-31).

3. It is forbidden to listen to a false prophet who tells the people to follow other gods, even if he gives signs and performs miracles. The false prophet must be executed (Deut. 13:2-6).

4. One may not even listen to one's own blood brother, son, daughter, wife or dearest friend, let alone anyone else, if they seek to seduce one to idolatry. The inciter must be executed (Deut 13: 7-12).

5. Where a majority of a city have been led astray into idolatry, all who took part in idol-worship must be put to the sword, and the entire city with all the people's possessions must be burned, never to be rebuilt (Deut. 13:13-19).

Misplaced zealotry

The very severity of the penalties for idolatry indicates just how serious a transgression it is. Yet this cannot justify zealots intoxicated with what they imagine to be their passionate love of God in feeling entitled and obliged to uproot and destroy everything they consider idolatrous. In our time we see almost daily reports of attacks and terrorist atrocities directed by members of various radical groups against synagogues, churches, mosques and temples belonging to anyone whom they consider idolatrous. Even the 9/11 attack on the New York World Trade Center, which claimed the lives of thousands of innocent citizens, was justified by certain fanatics as a "strike against idolatry".

But the truth is that the Torah enjoins the greatest caution in the practical application of the laws against idolatry, which is and must be subject to the authority of the Sanhedrin - the Supreme

Court of Torah law - and, in the case of the gentile nations, to duly constituted Noahide courts of law (Maimonides, Laws of Kings 9:14).

Investigate diligently

The very great caution with which we are to examine and investigate reports of possible breaches of the prohibition against idolatry is emphasized in our portion in the case of the commandment relating to the idolatrous city, where the Torah says:

"If you hear that in one of your cities. certain base men have gone forth and drawn away the inhabitants...**then you shall inquire and investtigate and ask diligently** , and if the matter is true and certain...you shall surely smite the inhabitants of that city".

Deuteronomy 13:15

The Torah uses an almost identical expression in next week's Torah portion, in the case of a man or a woman who goes and worships idols:

And if you are told or hear about this, **then you shall inquire diligently**, and if the matter is true and certain... you shall bring forth that man or woman... that they die.

Deuteronomy 17:4-5

In each of the above two passages, the Hebrew word for "inquire" is **vederashta**. Besides these two passages, this Hebrew word appears in only one other place in all the Five Books of Moses - also in next week's portion, where we are commanded to consult the Sanhedrin and inquire about all legal questions that we ourselves are not competent to determine:

If a matter of judgment arises that is too hard for you... you must get up and go... and come to the priests, the Levites and to the judge that will be in those days, and **you shall inquire**, and they shall declare to you the sentence of judgment."

Deuteronomy 17:8-9

"Inquire and receive a reward"

It is noteworthy that the legal requirements that would make an idolatrous city liable to destruction are so stringent that in actual fact, there was never a case where this law was put into effect, and nor will there ever be, as the Torah sages explicitly stated in the Talmud (Bavli, Sanhedrin 71a).

"If so," they asked, "why was this portion written in the Torah?" The sages answered: "Inquire and receive a reward!" (ibid.). In other words, our paramount duty is to study and internalize these Torah laws.

We see that the intent of the Torah is not that laymen and zealots should superficially read some texts and then furiously and indiscriminately rush to take the law into their own hands. Only the Sanhedrin or a duly constituted gentile Noahide court established in accordance with Moses' Torah is competent to determine what is or is not idolatry and where, if at all the death penalty applies.

The obligation of regular citizens is not to try to police the world but to inquire, investigate and study the Torah in order to constantly deepen and enhance their personal fulfillment of God's commandments, and to peacefully propagate among those around them the joyous Torah path and the love of HaShem, the One True God.

How to Make War

The Hebrew root **shalom**, which means **peace**, appears 887 times in the Torah, Prophets and Holy Writings. By contrast, the Hebrew root **lacham** in the sense of warfare appears no more than 576 times. This shows that **peace** is the highest value in the Torah, the ultimate good.

God promised Abraham he would come to his fathers in **peace** (Genesis 15:15). Joseph blessed Pharaoh with **peace** (Gen. 45:27). Jethro sent Moses away in **peace** (Exodus 4:18) and greeted him in **peace** (Ex. 18:7). The standard Hebrew greeting is **peace** (Genesis 29:6; 45:27; Esther 9:30). One of God's greatest blessings is **peace** in the land (Leviticus 26:6). God gave Pinchas His covenant of **peace** (Numbers 25:12). The priests bless the people with **peace** (Num. 6:26).

Bloodshed began when Cain killed Abel (Genesis 4:8). It was in the sixth generation of Cain's descendants that Tubal Cain - named after his ignominious ancestor - became "the forger of every cutting instrument of brass and iron" (Gen. 4:22) - i.e. the weapons of war.

The Torah abhorrence of the folly of war is apparent in the prophetic vision of the Age of Messiah: "They shall beat their swords into plow-shares and their spears into pruning-hooks, and nation will not raise the sword against nation, and **they shall no longer learn war**" (Isaiah 2:4).

A fact of life

Yet until the time of Messiah we live in a world where war is one of the facts of life. We therefore need to know how the Torah teaches us to make war when this is necessary.

The Torah gives man the inviolable right to self-defense: "If someone comes to kill you, get up and kill him first" (Talmud Bavli, Berachot 5a based on Exodus 22:1).

The Torah gives explicit lessons on warfare in our present portion of **Shoftim**, whose laws are mainly concerned with the judiciary, kingship, priesthood and government, who are charged with responsibility in matters of state:

"When you go forth to war against your enemies. do not fear them, for HaShem your God is with you. Hear O Israel: HaShem is your God. When you draw close to a city to fight against it, then call them to **peace**."

Deuteronomy 20 vv. 1, 3-4, 10

Israel were commanded to make war against certain nations, and much of the history told in the Bible concerns Israel's various wars. This has led some to slander Israel as if the Torah glorifies warfare and conquest, but that is a fallacy and a distortion. The actual number of wars recorded in the Bible during the 1390 years from the birth of Abraham (1812 B.C.E.) until the destruction of King Solomon's Temple (422 B.C.E.) is small compared to the numbers of wars that have gripped the world incessantly in later times.

Israel were explicitly commanded not to wage war against certain neighboring peoples such as Edom (Deut. 2:4-5), Moab (Deut 2:9) and Ammon (Deut 2:19). Israel could only fight these peoples if they attacked.

The only nations against whom Israel were commanded to wage war were the Amalekites - inveterate, unrepentant terrorist killers (Deuteronomy 25:17-19) - and the Seven Canaanite Nations, who were irredeemably corrupt idol-worshipers (Leviticus 20:18). Even so, before attacking them, Israel were first to invite them to make **peace**.

"When you draw close to a city to fight against it, then call them to **peace**. But if they will not make peace with you but they make war against you, then you shall besiege them."

Deuteronomy 20 vv 10, 12

God's witnesses

The wars commanded by the Torah do not have the same goal as most of the wars that have been waged historically by the various nations, whose primary purpose has been to conquer others in order to gain more and better territories, wealth and resources.

Israel's purpose is not mere territorial control but to serve as God's witnesses (Isaiah 43:10) and to radiate the light of His Torah to the nations in order to bring them to the knowledge of God. When Israel pursue this purpose through warfare, where this is necessary, the priest can truly tell them that they have no need to fear, "for it is HaShem your God who goes with you to fight for you against your enemies in order to deliver you" (Deuteronomy 20:4).

The call to **peace** that Israel are commanded to make to their adversaries before commencing battle is a call for them to accept upon themselves the Seven Noahide Commandments that apply to all humanity. If they do so, all of them are spared without exception (Maimonides, Mishneh Torah, Laws of Kings 6:1).

"And it shall be, if they give you the answer of peace and open up to you, then it shall be that all the people that are found therein shall become tributary to you and serve you."

Deuteronomy 20:11

Historically, in almost all cases where one nation conquered and subjugated another, the victors willfully and mercilessly humiliated and exploited the subject people.

But the tributary status of nations that make peace with Israel on Israel's terms - acceptance of the Seven Noahide Commandments - is actually the greatest honor, as these nations thereby become attached to the service of the One God - for Israel are nothing but His servants (Leviticus 25:42) and their national mission is only to glorify Him (Isaiah 49:3).

Do not wantonly destroy

If the enemy refuse to make peace, Israel are permitted to make war against them even if it means laying siege against them until they die of starvation, thirst or disease, because if they refrain, the enemy will sooner or later fight against them (Rashi on Deut. 20:12).

Yet the Torah places a most important limit on "all-out war":

"When you besiege a city for a long time in making war against it to take it, you may not destroy its trees by wielding an axe against them. You may eat from them, but you may not cut them down. For is the tree of the field man, that it should be under siege from you?

"Only the trees which you know not to be trees giving food, may you destroy and cut down in order to build bulwarks against the city that makes war against you until it falls."

Deuteronomy 20:19-20

One of the classic military strategies that has characterized many wars until today is the "scorched earth" policy, which involves destroying anything that might be useful to the enemy while advancing or withdrawing from an area. A notorious example of this was the deliberate burning of the oil fields of Kuwait by the retreating Iraqi army under orders from Saddam Hussein in the First Gulf War (1991).

This is forbidden under the 1977 Geneva Conventions (Protocol I Article 54):

It is prohibited to attack, destroy, remove, or render useless objects indispensable to the survival of the civilian population, such as foodstuffs, agricultural areas for the production of foodstuffs, crops, livestock, drinking water installations and supplies, and irrigation works, for the specific purpose of denying them for their sustenance value to the civilian population or to the adverse Party, whatever the motive, whether in order to starve out civilians, to cause them to move away, or for any other motive.

This prohibition is clearly rooted in the Torah prohibition against willfully destroying useful resources.

But despite being prohibited, it is still a common practice.

Besides being prohibited in the heat of war, the destruction of useful resources - even unwanted household utensils and the like, or even edible food that could be used for animal feed, compost etc. - is also included in the Torah prohibition against wanton destruction, which applies not only to "fruit trees" but to all items that could potentially be of use.

We need to take this prohibition with the utmost seriousness in an age when growing populations across the world combined with global economic recession and widespread poverty are making the value of scant resources ever more apparent.

The Home Front

Our portion of **Ki Teitzei** opens with the words: "When you go out war against your enemies." (Deuteronomy 21:10).

Which war is this talking about? An earlier section of the Torah in the previous portion began with the very same words: "When you go out to war against your enemies and you see horses and chariots and people more numerous than you" (Deuteronomy 10:1). In that section the Torah is obviously speaking about how to conduct military war literally on the battlefield.

But in our present portion the Torah addresses a different kind of war. This is the war that takes place *after* the battle against military enemies has been won. "When you go out to war against your enemies and HaShem your God delivers them into your hands and you take them captive, and you see among the captives a woman of beautiful form and you desire her and take her as your wife: **you shall bring her inside your home...**" (Deut. 21:10-12).

War on the home front

The "warfare" that is the common denominator in almost all of the many varied laws contained in our present portion is on a different level from that of military war. In our portion, the war is **inside the home** and inside our very selves. Even in times of peace, we are constantly confronted by an enemy that is not an obvious military enemy. Rather, this is the enemy that dwells in the heart of each one of us from very childhood, an enemy that even poses as our friend! This is the "evil inclination" that God implants in each one, which at every juncture in life prompts, urges and nags us to follow our selfish materialistic desires for perceived personal gain and gratification rather than to do what is right and proper in accordance with the Torah. If we show strength and discipline in restraining and controlling this enemy, God may grant us victory so that we bring our lives under the rule of the "good inclination" in order to merit His great reward in the life after life for all who follow His laws.

The "beautiful captive" as a symbol

The "beautiful captive" who is the subject of the first law in this portion may be seen as the embodiment of beautiful and alluring aspects of the wider materialistic world that surrounds us. We may desire to "capture" them and bring them inside our homes and incorporate them into our lives in the hope that we may enjoy them while still keeping them under control so as not allow them to deflect us from our true purpose of serving the One God. However, the rabbis urged great caution, teaching that such "marriages" may lead to disastrous consequences, as when things go sour (symbolized in the domestic strife and hatred and the rebellious child that are the subjects of the ensuing verses in this section, Deuteronomy 21:14-21).

In our times, one of the ways the "enemy" can invade our homes and penetrate our very minds and hearts is through the television, newspapers and magazines, and Internet - which expose us to all the allure of the surrounding world inside our very living rooms, consciously or unconsciously influencing our minds, thoughts, feelings and opinions in all areas of life.

Teachings for daily life

The rabbis enumerated a total of 72 separate commandments given to Israel in our present portion of **Ki Teitzei**. The earlier portions in Deuteronomy contain many laws relating to the prohibition of idolatry, the Temple, festivals, judiciary, kingship and government. In marked contrast, almost all of the commandments in **Ki Teitzei** relate to the lives of ordinary men and women in the home, at work, in business, in marriage, raising children and dealing with all kinds of matters that come up in everyday life - from returning lost property (Deut. 22:1-3) to standards of dress (ibid. v. 5) and general safety (ibid. v. 8).

Some of the specifics in the laws in this portion may appear to relate to an agrarian world that has largely gone by for those concentrated in today's mammoth urban agglomerations, where it is most unlikely to find someone's lost ox or lamb (Deut. 22:1) or to be picking grapes in their vineyard (23:25).

Yet while cast in terms of life in the ancient Biblical world, many of these laws have important applications even in our slick, sophisticated modern world, which suffers too much from cases of adultery, rape and seduction (Deut. 22:13-29), kidnapping (Deut. 24:7), physical assault (Deut. ch. 25 v 3 & vv 11-12) and other evils. The Torah forbids exploiting wage-laborers and other poor people or delaying payment of their wages (Deut. 24:14-15). It forbids creditors from confiscating vital possessions from defaulting debtors (Deut. 24:10-13). On the contrary, the Torah teaches that we must keep in mind the needs of the poor and underprivileged even as we reap the gains we have earned through our own efforts (Deut. 24:19-21). We must be scrupulously honest at work and in business, and the weights and measures we use in buying and selling must be accurate (Deut. 25:13-16). If we are prohibited from employing "double standards" in business, the same must surely apply to the standards with which we "measure" and judge people's behavior. It is wrong to apply stricter standards to those we dislike and more lenient standards to those we favor.

Each area of life presents its own challenges, with opportunities to follow the Torah in the way we respond or fall into possible pitfalls if we follow the promptings of the evil inclination. In strengthening ourselves in the daily war against the evil inclination, we must exercise the greatest caution in who or what we admit inside our own homes and within the inner sanctum of our minds and hearts lest we allow negative influences to hold sway over us and deprive us of the rewards that come from following the path of God in our lives.

Reward and Punishment

In the portion of **Ki Tavo** Moses completes his exposition of the commandments of the Torah, after which he launches into his final reproofs to Israel prior to leaving the life of this world.

Almost the last of the commandments given in the Torah are set forth in our portion:

(1) Thanksgiving over presenting the First Fruits to the priest in the Temple (Deut. 26:1-11), where we acknowledge G-d for blessing the work of our hands.

(2) The Declaration over having given the proper tithes from our livelihood (Deut. 26:12-15), where we affirm before God that not only do we seek to feed ourselves, but we also share what we have with the needy - the Levite, whose whole life is dedicated to God, the alien resident, the orphan and the widow.

Written on stone

Prior to the Children of Israel's entry into their ancestral Promised Land under Moses' destined successor, Joshua, Moses instructed them to carry out a special ceremony immediately after their crossing the River Jordan into the Land. In this ceremony they were to take great stones, coat them with white lime, and write on them the entire Torah in all of the Seventy Languages of the root nations of the world (Deuteronomy 27:1-8, see Rashi on v. 8). All the Twelve Tribes of Israel were then to assemble at the twin mountains of Gerizim and Eival, where the Levites were to administer a unique oath cursing anyone who would flout the fundamental laws of the Torah.

If this ceremony came only to bind Israel to the Torah it might have been sufficient for them to write the Torah in their own native language of Hebrew and none other. But the fact that they were to write it in all the Seventy Languages indicates that all the peoples of the world are to learn lessons from the Torah.

Reward and Punishment

One of the most important lessons for all people contained in the portion of **Ki Tavo** is that "HaShem is righteous in all His ways" (Psalms 145:17). The commandments of the Torah are not merely good advice that we are at liberty to embrace or reject without consequences one way or the other. Rather, they are God's Laws for all the world. As with every system of laws, there are benefits from observing them and sanctions and penalties for infringing them. The catalog of rich blessings that God will send to Israel for keeping His commandments (Deuteronomy 28:1-14) and the dreadful curses if they rebel (ibid. 14-69) comes to demonstrate the axiomatic truth that God deals with perfect righteousness to all, whether righteous or wicked.

In the words of Abraham:

It is far from You to act in this manner, to slay the righteous with the wicked, so that the righteous should be like the wicked. That is far from You; shall not the Judge of all the earth do justly?

Genesis 18:25

Thus the sages of Israel taught that "the Holy One, blessed be He, does not withhold the reward of any of His creatures" (Pesachim 118a). This is said to apply even to animals, and how much more so to human beings, who have free will to choose whether to do good deeds or bad.

Even the wicked are rewarded for their good deeds. Thus, even Nebuchadnezzar the evil king of Babylon was awarded the booty and plunder of Egypt in reward for his having carried out God's will in besieging Tyre (Ezekiel 29:18-20).

The wicked are rewarded materially in this world for any good they may do - in order that after having eaten their reward in this life, they then lose the bliss of the life eternal that is reserved for the righteous. This principle is stated earlier in Deuteronomy:

"Know therefore that HaShem your G-d, He is G-d; the faithful G-d, who keeps the covenant and mercy with those who love Him and keep His commandments to a thousand generations; and repays those who hate Him to their face, to destroy them; He will not be slack to one that hates Him, He will repay him to his face."

Deuteronomy 7:9-10, see Rashi on v. 10

Thus after their great glory in this world, the wicked are depicted by the prophets as descending into hell:

Isaiah 14:4-20 depicts the horror of the inhabitants of the nether world in seeing Nebuchadnezzar, "the man who made the earth tremble, who shook kingdoms", cast down to the bottom of the pit like a carcass trodden under foot. Likewise Isaiah 30:31-33 depicts a deep, large hearth kindled with a stream of brimstone to punish Sennacherib king of Assyria. Similarly Ezekiel 32:17-32 depicts all the villainous nations of the earth and their kings and princes in their "graves" in the farthest depths of the pit in punishment for their having caused terror in the land of the living.

The righteous of the nations

Even where God has decreed that certain nations must take a wicked role in history, he does not decree on any specific member of those nations to be among the wicked, for each individual is free to refrain from doing evil if he so desires (Maimonides, Laws of Repentance 6:5). Every person in the world is at liberty to opt out of the surrounding wickedness and to "guard the way of HaShem to practice charity and justice" (Genesis 18:19).

Thus "everyone who accepts the Seven Command-ments [of the Children of Noah] and is careful to practice them is among the Righteous of the Nations of the world and has a share in the World to Come" (Maimonides, Laws of Kings 8:11).

It must be understood that God's reward for observance of the Torah, whether by the Children of Israel or by the Righteous of the Nations, may not be visible at all in this world, where it seems that often the righteous suffer while the wicked apparently prosper.

But it is an article of Torah faith that this deceptive world in which we live is not the world of reward. Rather, it is the testing ground for our souls amidst all our different trials and temptations here, in order that we should endeavor to follow the path of God's law despite all obstacles, and thereby attain His true reward in the life after life.

Thus the Talmud relates that Rabbi Joseph, the son of Rabbi Joshua ben Levy, fell sick and expired in what might be seen as a case of a clinical death experience. When Rabbi Joseph came back to life, his father asked him: "What did you see?" He replied, "I saw an opposite world: those who are superior here are insignificant there, whereas those who lowly here are superior there!" His father answered: "What you saw there is a pure world" (Pesachim 50a).

The Good of the World to Come

In the words of Rabbi Nachman of Breslov:

We call the reward in the World to Come "good" because there is simply no other term to describe it. Yet even the word "good" is quite inadequate, because this reward is far beyond good. Still, the only way to explain it to people is by calling it good, although in truth, "no eye has seen it, other than God" (Isaiah 64:3; Rabbi Nachman's Wisdom #55).

The reward each one attains depends entirely on his or her efforts. For "according to the effort, so is the reward" (Ethics of the Fathers 5:22). Even if a person has done much evil, they need not despair, for the path of repentance is always open.

Lessons of the Land

As the Five Books of the Torah approach their triumphant conclusion, Moses prophesies that the very Land of Israel itself will teach a stark lesson both to Israel and also to all the people of the world:

Lest there be among you a man or woman or family or tribe whose heart turns away today from HaShem our God to go to serve the gods of those nations. and when he hears the words of this curse, he will bless himself in his heart, saying: 'I shall have peace, even though I walk in the stubbornness of my heart'. HaShem will not be willing to pardon him, but then the anger of HaShem and His jealousy shall be kindled against that man.

And the generation to come, your children that shall arise after you, **and the foreigner that shall come from a far land** , shall say, when they see the plagues of that land and the sicknesses with which HaShem has afflicted it, and that the whole land is brimstone, salt and burning which is not sown and does not bear, nor does any grass grow in it, like the overthrow of Sodom and Gomorrah, Admah and Zeboiim, which HaShem overthrew in His anger and in His wrath; **even all**

the nations shall say 'Why has HaShem done this to this land? What is the meaning of the heat of this great anger?' Then men shall say: 'Because they forsook the covenant of HaShem, the God of their fathers, which He made with them when He brought them out of the land of Egypt, and they went and served other gods and worshipped them, gods that they did not know, and that He had not allotted to them; therefore the anger of HaShem was kindled against this land, to bring upon it all the curse that is written in this book.'

Deuteronomy 29:17-26

The truth of Moses' prophecy is borne out by the fact that during nearly two thousand years when most of the people of Israel were in exile following the destruction of the Second Temple in 70 C.E., their Land lay forbiddingly barren and desolate. We have vivid testimony to HaShem's venting His anger on the Land in the writings of the famous American author Mark Twain (1835-1910), who came as a "foreigner from a far land" to visit Israel, then known as Palestine, in the year 1867. Afterwards he described what he found:

"The hills are barren, they are dull of color. The valleys are unsightly deserts fringed with a feeble vegetation that has an expression about it of being sorrowful and despondent. Every outline is harsh. It is a hopeless, dreary, heart-broken land. Palestine sits in sackcloth and ashes. Over it broods the spell of a curse that has withered its

fields and fettered its energies. Renowned Jerusalem itself, the stateliest name in history, has lost
all its ancient grandeur, and is become a pauper
village; the riches of Solomon are no longer there
to compel the admiration of visiting Oriental
queens. Palestine is desolate and unlovely. And
why should it be otherwise? Can the curse of the
Deity beautify a land?" Mark Twain, "Innocents
Abroad" chapter 56

Yet just a few years after Mark Twain's visit to the
Holy Land, there began the enormous influx of
Jewish immigrants who returned to their ancestral
land in great waves from the 1870's until the
present. Within a few generations, the land of
Israel has been transformed into a busy, flourishing, astonishingly fertile country that exports
luscious fruits and agricultural know-how as well as
leading hi-tech and other products to countries all
over the world. It is a fact that in the "Land of Milk
and Honey", the very cows provide higher yields of
milk than in any other country in the world, while
cuttings of date palms imported from other lands
for planting in Israel produce fatter, more succu-
lent honey dates than in the lands of origin of the
mother trees! (Asaph Goor, "Fruits of the Holy
Land").

For in the same prophecy of Moses quoted above,
HaShem promised:

'And it shall come to pass when all these things
have come upon you, the blessing and the
curse... then HaShem thy God will turn your

captivity and have compassion upon you, and will return and gather you from all the peoples where HaShem your God has scattered you. And HaShem your God will bring you into the land which your fathers possessed, and you shall possess it. And HaShem your God will make you over-abundant in all the work of your hand, in the fruit of your body and in the fruit of your cattle and in the fruit of your land, for good. If you will listen to the voice of HaShem your God to keep His commandments and His statutes which are written in this book of the law; if you turn to HaShem your God with all your heart and with all your soul.'

Deuteronomy 30:1, 3, 5, 9-10

Moses words, delivered three and a half millennia ago, are a clear warning to the people of Israel to keep the Torah in order to avoid God's terrible curses and receive His rich blessings.

What is the message for the gentile, the "stranger from a far-off land", whom the Torah also calls to testify that the curse was visited on the Land because the Children of Israel forsook God's Covenant?

Surely the Torah comes to teach all people that the very Land of Israel bears witness to God's flawless Justice in "preserving all who love him; but all the wicked He will destroy" (Psalms 145:20).

There may exist "a man or woman... whose heart turns away today from HaShem... and when he hears the words of this curse, he will bless himself in his heart, saying: 'I shall have peace, even though I walk in the stubbornness of my heart...' (Deut. 29:17-18). People may persuade themselves that they can violate God's laws and escape the consequences. But the testimony of the very Land itself, the testimony of History, is that 'HaShem will not be willing to pardon him, but then the anger of HaShem and His jealousy shall be kindled against that man' (ibid.).

This applies both to the Israelites - who are obligated to observe the 613 Commandments of the Torah - and to the Gentiles, who are commanded to follow the Seven Laws of the Children of Noah.

'I have set before you life and death, the blessing and the curse; therefore choose life, that you may live, you and your offspring.'

Deuteronomy 30:19

Moses' Last Song

For I proclaim the name of HaShem; ascribe greatness to our God! (Deuteronomy 32:3).

Moses' entire mission was to "proclaim the name of HaShem", teaching His ways and His laws to Israel and to all the peoples of the world.

On the last day of his life in this world, Moses taught the Children of Israel his final "song" - the affirmation of HaShem's perfect justice:

"The Rock, His work is perfect; for all His ways are justice; a God of faithfulness and without iniquity, just and right is He.

"Is corruption His? No; His children's is the blemish; a generation crooked and perverse" (verses 4-5).

People may rail against God for what they imagine to be His injustices, but in most cases they themselves have caused of their own afflictions. In the words of King Solomon: "Man's foolishness perverts his way, yet his heart rages against HaShem" (Proverbs 19:3).

Moses' song applies both to Israel and to all humanity, for their destinies are inextricably intertwined.

"Remember the days of old, consider the years of many generations; ask your father, and he will explain to you, your elders, and they will tell you. When the Most High gave to the nations their inheritance, when He separated the children of men, He set the borders of the peoples according to the number of the children of Israel. For HaShem's portion is His people, Jacob the lot of His inheritance" (verses 7-9).

God chose Israel as His witnesses, and He "set the borders of the peoples according to the number of the Children of Israel". Among the various implications contained in these words is that the habitations of the Children of Israel, whether in their own or in other lands, are far from arbitrary. Rather, they have been sent on a mission to proclaim HaShem to all the different peoples of the world, each within their own "borders" and boundaries, geographical, racial, cultural and ideological.

Moses' song warns the Children of Israel not to rebel against their mission, for God would surely punish them, withdrawing His protection so as to leave them vulnerable to the ravages of their enemies and God's avenging forces.

Yet even if the Children of Israel sin, the nations may not use this as an excuse for themselves to sin. Everyone in the world must acknowledge and submit to HaShem, for nobody can escape His hand:

"See now that I, even I, am He, and there is no god with Me; I kill, and I make alive; I have wounded, and I heal; and there is none that can deliver out of My hand" (verse 39).

No-one can escape God's vengeance against those who violate His laws:

"For I lift up My hand to heaven, and say: 'As I live forever, if I whet My flashing sword, and My hand take hold on judgment; I will render vengeance to My adversaries, and will recompense those that hate Me. I will make My arrows drunk with blood, and My sword shall devour flesh, with the blood of the slain and the captives, from the long-haired heads of the enemy.'

"Sing aloud, O ye nations, of His people; for He avenges the blood of His servants, and renders vengeance to His adversaries, and makes expiation for the land of His people" (verses 40-43).

We cannot but discern God's hand of judgment and vengeance in the turmoil afflicting today's world in fulfillment of Zechariah's prophecy of the End of Days:

"And it shall come to pass in that day, that a great tumult from HaShem shall be among them; and they shall lay hold every one on the hand of his neighbor, and his hand shall rise up against the hand of his neighbour" (Zechariah 14:13).

Today we see a raging multi-front war of cultures being waged in the very streets of Europe and America between "Islam" and "the West" and between "Traditionalism" and "Permissiveness".

We see actual and looming wars in the Middle East, Asia, Africa and the Americas that threaten to drag in more and more countries, with the potential to turn into a veritable World War that could dwarf all previous wars.

Peace will only come to the world when all humanity submit themselves to HaShem and embrace His Torah - whose "ways are ways of pleasantness and all of whose paths are peace" (Proverbs 3:17). Israel must repent and return to the practice of their 613 Commandments, and all the other peoples must repent and practice the Seven Noahide Laws. This is the only way left.

Let us search and investigate our ways, and return to HaShem (Lamentations 3:40).

Moses Lives

"And Moses, servant of HaShem, died there in the land of Moab by the mouth of HaShem. And He buried him in the valley in the land of Moab over against Beth Pe'or, and no man knows his burial place to this day."

Deuteronomy 34:5-6

"...and there are those who say that Moses did not die, because here (Deuteronomy 34:5) it is written: 'And Moses died', but there it is written: 'And he was there [on Mount Sinai] with HaShem for forty days and forty nights' (Exodus 34:28). Just as there it means he was standing and ministering, so here it means he stands and ministers."

Babylonian Talmud, Sotah 13b

"The righteous are greater after their death than in their lifetime."

Babylonian Talmud, Chullin 7b

The biblical verse explicitly states that Moses died -- for none of Adam's descendants are exempt from the decree of death (Genesis 3:19). Yet the Torah sages could not believe that the man who was so pure that he stood at Sinai for forty days ministering before the Living God simply underwent the same kind of ignominious death and decay as ordinary people. Indeed, until today Moses' physical body has never been discovered, as the Torah itself testifies. Yet as the Master of all the prophets and the chief lawgiver of mono-theism, Moses' influence endures until today through the Torah of Israel and all who uphold it, as well as indirectly through Christianity, Islam and many other influences in our culture that are ultimately rooted in the Torah.

If Moses is "dead" - a figure from the past that has no bearing on the present - this is only from the limited perspective of fallible humans, who often imagine that only those who are in a living, physical body can be considered "alive". They cannot grasp that the souls of the righteous are very much alive in the spiritual realm, which indeed permeates the physical world in which we live, influencing it in a multitude of unseen ways.

To those who follow the Torah, which is "the Tree of Life for those who take hold of it" (Proverbs 3:18), Moses is very much alive and a source of guidance and inspiration in our world today. Moses is only "dead" to those who do not hear the call of the Torah - or do not wish to hear it.

Some who claim to speak in the name of Christianity say that "the Jews killed God" – a ludicrous thought, since God is not a corporeal being that anyone could "kill". A similar accusation can be turned against those very people for trying to "kill" Moses with the idea that the Torah of Israel that he brought into the world had in some way become defunct. But at HaShem's dictation, Moses testified that the Torah is eternal and cannot be changed in any way: "You shall not add to it or subtract from it" (Deut. 13:1). Indeed, the Christian scriptures acknowledge that "not the smallest letter or one dot will disappear from the Law …" but in actual fact in the Christian world there has been a widespread tendency to ignore or even actively discourage its practice. Most Jews who converted to Christianity abandoned their Torah observance even though the Law never was and never could be abrogated.

Likewise, some who claim to speak in the name of Islam relate their tradition to Biblical personalities and teachings yet imply that Moses' prophecy was in some sense superseded by that of their prophet, despite the fact that the latter stated that he heard from an angel, while Moses heard from the mouth of HaShem (Numbers 12:8). Some claiming to speak in the name of Islam state that "the Jews manipulated their texts". But this is a slander, as is clear to anyone who is familiar with the strict rules governing the writing of Torah scrolls to ensure that each one is an exact copy of a copy of a copy of Moses' original Torah scroll that was kept with the Ark of the Covenant in the Temple. With Jews so often prone to argue with one another about almost everything, how could any one person have persuaded everyone else that his was the authentic

Torah text if not Moses himself, whom all Israel accepted as HaShem's greatest prophet?

The fact is that although the Torah scroll must be handwritten by a scribe and contains a total of 304,805 Hebrew letters, all the Torah scrolls in the world are identical with the exception of certain scrolls from Jewish communities in Yemen that have only 9 cases of different spellings, which do not affect the meaning of the original. This contrasts with the number of textual variants in copies of the "New Testament", of which the lowest estimate is around 30,000, while there is abundant evidence that the Quran underwent textual corruption via additions, omissions and conflicting variant readings.

Any tradition that denies the authenticity of the Torah as HaShem's word revealed to Moses is immediately vulnerable to more serious doubts about its own sources. For "HaShem is not a man that He should lie" (Numbers 23:13). If HaShem's eternal Torah could somehow be changed or abrogated, what would give any other tradition immunity against forgery and abrogation?

Yet the truth of the Torah cannot be "proved" through argument and external proofs. The only way to know and experience the truth of the Torah is through persistent, careful study. "*Taste* and see that HaShem is good; happy is the man that trusts in Him" (Psalms 34:9).

Moses lives on in the Torah which he brought to the world at HaShem's dictation. Until today, Moses' influence is a blessing to all who devote themselves to the study and practice of the Torah.

"And this is the blessing which Moses, the man of God, blessed..."

Deuteronomy 33:1

www.ingramcontent.com/pod-product-compliance
Lightning Source LLC
Chambersburg PA
CBHW052031090426
42739CB00010B/1859